100 GREAT LEADING WELL IDEAS

GREAT
LEADING WELL
IDEAS

Dr Peter Shaw

Marshall Cavendish
Business

© 2017 Peter Shaw

Published by Marshall Cavendish Business
An imprint of Marshall Cavendish International
1 New Industrial Road, Singapore 536196

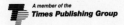
A member of the
Times Publishing Group

Other Marshall Cavendish Offices:

Marshall Cavendish Corporation. 99 White Plains Road, Tarrytown NY 10591-9001, USA • Marshall Cavendish International (Thailand) Co Ltd. 253 Asoke, 12th Flr, Sukhumvit 21 Road, Klongtoey Nua, Wattana, Bangkok 10110, Thailand • Marshall Cavendish (Malaysia) Sdn Bhd, Times Subang, Lot 46, Subang Hi-Tech Industrial Park, Batu Tiga, 40000 Shah Alam, Selangor Darul Ehsan, Malaysia

Marshall Cavendish is a registered trademark of Times Publishing Limited

National Library Board, Singapore Cataloguing in Publication Data
Names: Shaw, Peter.
Title: 100 great leading well ideas / Peter Shaw.
Description: Singapore : Marshall Cavendish Business, [2017]
Identifiers: OCN 967917599 | 978-981-4771-03-0 (paperback)
Subjects: LCSH: Leadership. | Industrial management.
Classification: DDC 658.4092—dc23

Printed in Singapore by JCS Digital Solutions Pte Ltd

This book is dedicated to all the individuals and teams
I have had the privilege to coach, with thanks to them
for the joy and fulfilment they have given me.

CONTENTS

SECTION C: Who?

SECTION D: How?

SECTION E: When?

SECTION F: Which?

SECTION G: Where?

SECTION H: Be

SECTION I: Become

SECTION J: Know

ACKNOWLEDGEMENTS

IT HAS BEEN A JOY to write this book during the summer of 2016. My elder son, Graham, suggested I write a book which sets out what I think are the key ingredients to leading well. I have sought to draw from my first career working in the public sector for 32 years and then a second career working in the private sector for 14 years, alongside a variety of roles within the voluntary sector.

It has been a privilege to draw from the experience of working with leaders across six continents in a wide range of settings. In the last few months I have worked with the United Nations' leadership team in Zambia, which included leaders of UN organisations from eight different nations. I also led three week-long workshops at Regent College in Vancouver, Canada, which included participants from 12 different nations around the Pacific.

I am indebted to many people for allowing me to share their leadership journeys. I am grateful to my colleagues at Praesta Partners for their stimulus in thinking through how best we can coach people to lead well in a variety of contexts. Jackie Tookey has typed the manuscript with her normal wonderful cheerfulness and efficiency. Sonia John-Lewis managed my diary and time effectively in order to enable me to write this book. Tracy Easthope has very willingly and skilfully taken over managing my diary to enable me to continue to coach, write and teach. Melvin Neo has been a thoughtful editor of this series and Mike Spilling has been an admirable editor of this book.

I am grateful to Chris Hopson who has written the foreword to the book. Chris and I have worked closely together over the last twelve years and have had many conversations about what leading well means. Chris has been a source of insight and practical good sense to many leaders in the health world in recent years drawing from the wealth of his experiences in a variety of leadership roles.

Frances, my wife, has been hugely supportive during the writing of this and the earlier books. I know that I can always have constructive conversations about leadership issues with my children and their delightful and thoughtful spouses, Anna, Owen and Holly. Graham gave me the idea for the book. Ruth, a superb planner, is always supportive and encouraging, with Colin always being a source of interesting ideas.

I hope that you, the reader, enjoy dipping into the ideas in the book. Each section includes a hypothetical character, except Section A, which is autobiographical. I hope that the different sections provide the reader with useful prompts about what leading well means for them going forward.

FOREWORD

IN MY EXPERIENCE, leading well is a skill we develop over time. Being a good leader is a never ending journey where we learn as much from what we've got wrong as what we've got right.

I've been lucky enough to have had Peter as a friend, guide and mentor on my leadership journey. As you will see from the pages that follow, Peter is wise and thoughtful on what it takes to lead well.

His book is an admirable source of sound, practical, advice which is highly relevant to leaders in any sphere, whatever your role, sector or nationality. It is full of common sense, encouraging you to expand your comfort zone, be clear about your expectations of yourself and others, and take responsibility for setting the culture and standards that ensure your team succeeds.

As I reflect on my own leadership journey so far, three lessons stand out.

First, be ruthless on how you prioritise your time. Every leadership role has many demands but focus most on what only you can do.

Second, however good you think you are, you can only deliver through others. Set a clear direction, delegate well and be available as a mentor and guide, with a particular emphasis on creating the next generation of leaders to follow you.

Third, seek out and then act on feedback. We spend a lot of time seeking to be evidence based in our leadership actions. Feedback from others is the best evidence on our own performance and we should act accordingly.

I hope you will find Peter's wisdom and insight as useful as I have done. I'd encourage you to read the book with an open mind, ready to learn and then experiment as you engage with the challenges you will face as a leader and manager.

Chris Hopson
Chief Executive
National Health Service Providers
London

INTRODUCTION

I STARTED WRITING THIS BOOK during the Rio Olympics of 2016 when the television screens were full of examples of individuals and teams who had prepared thoroughly for their Olympic events. The gold medallists were full of praise for those who had supported and challenged them. The involvement of the coaches in stretching the imaginations of participants was a key ingredient in the success of individuals and teams. My task in this book is to stretch your imagination about how to lead well.

I wrote my first book in this series, *100 Great Personal Impact Ideas*, during the London Olympics of 2012. During subsequent summers I wrote books in this same series: *100 Great Coaching Ideas*, *100 Great Team Effectiveness Ideas* and *100 Great Building Success Ideas*. This book, the fifth in the series, aims to bring together a coherent and comprehensive perspective on leading well. I deliberately cross-refer to other books and booklets I have written or co-authored to provide opportunity for further reflection about these themes.

I suggest that at the heart of leading well is asking the questions of 'Why?', 'What?', 'Who?', 'How?', 'When?', 'Which?' and 'Where?' I then look at how you want to 'Be' as an effective leader and then at what you want to 'Become' more capable at doing as you take on further leadership responsibilities. I conclude with looking at what you need to 'Know' about yourself as you build for your future.

This book is relevant to leaders in any sphere and at any stage in their lives. Reviewing how you lead well is just as important for the aspiring leader aged 25 as the experienced leader aged 75. I have deliberately sought to draw from the experience of working with leaders and leadership teams across six continents. The cultural background and expectations may be very different, but many of the requirements for leading well are the same.

The book is designed so you can dip into different sections. It is intended to be a practical tool both for individuals and for those mentoring younger people. My hope is that the ideas in the book provide you with prompts for thought and action as you review how you can lead well into future.

Canon Professor Peter Shaw, CB, PhD, DCL(Hon)
Godalming, England
peter.shaw@praesta.com

SECTION A
WHY?

UNDERSTAND WHY YOU WANT TO MAKE A DIFFERENCE

Understanding what is at the root of why you want to make a difference helps shape your intent and the values that underpin your actions.

The idea

An easy answer when someone is asked why they want to take on leadership responsibility is, 'I want to make a difference'. The good mentor will want to understand where the individual's motivation comes from and how deep-seated it is. Is it because the individual has inherited from their family or community a strong sense of purpose or values? Does the drive to make a difference come from a strong inner desire to do good, or does the drive result from an inner fear of inadequacy or failure?

It is worth pushing yourself to understand where your drive to make a difference comes from, and whether it is having a constructive or destructive effect on you. You might recognise that you have an inner compunction to climb every mountain before you. You might have, deep in your memory, words from your parents about their expectations of the contribution you would make as an adult. The more you understand why you have an inner drive to make a difference, the easier it is to focus that drive constructively and not allow it to overwhelm other priorities in your life.

See inner drives as potentially hugely constructive if they are focused in the right direction, while remain wary of their destructive effect if the desire to make a difference in one sphere crushes your humanity and contribution in other spheres.

Alan recognised that much of his inner drive came from his upbringing in a small, Yorkshire town. His father had died when Alan was seven: his mother had focused her energy on ensuring that Alan recovered from the sense of loss and moved through school into university at a time when a small proportion of young people went on to higher education. Alan's mother had been the first female, senior manager in a manufacturing plant in her early thirties, and had given up her career when she got married. Alan recognised that he had inherited from his mother a deeply embedded desire to carry forward her legacy of making a difference in the next generation.

In practice

- In what ways is a desire to make a difference rooted in you?

- What legacy has been passed down to you from your parents?

- What part did the community in which you grew up play in helping develop and shape a desire to make a difference?

- In what ways does the desire to make a difference in one sphere undermine how you move forward in other spheres of your life?

RECOGNISE THE FRAMEWORK YOU APPLY TO LEADING WELL

IF YOU CAN ARTICULATE clearly the framework you apply to leading well you can more readily observe yourself in a dispassionate way.

The idea

When I coach aspiring leaders I encourage them to articulate a clear framework covering the four Vs of leadership: vision, values, value-added and vitality. I believe these are the essential ingredients of effective leadership. I encourage them to think of these four Vs as the cornerstones of both their work and personal lives. I suggest that aspiring leaders think about their distinctive characteristics and how they want to build on those characteristics to develop a vision of who they want to be in their work, in their family and in their community. I prompt them to think about the values that shape and define them, and how those values can be harnessed to enable them to make a difference in their work and in their community. I encourage them to ensure their values are their biggest asset and not their worst liability.

My belief is that aspiring leaders should be continually reassessing the value-added contribution they can make. This starts from a clear appreciation of their unique strengths, and then clarity about how their strengths can be developed and used to best effect. It includes a recognition that the value-added contribution you made at one stage in your career has got you so far, but now needs to be developed into a different type of value-added contribution. For example, success at an early stage is all about your own individual contribution.

Your value-added contribution in the next stage may focus on enabling other people to do the detailed work in a co-ordinated and effective way.

The vitality strand is core to applying vision, value and value-added to best effect. Knowing the sources of vitality for any leader is at the heart of managing their energy and time well so they are continuing to bring a fresh approach that energises others.[1]

Alan had the benefit of a spell early in his career working as the private secretary to successive heads of Government Departments, which helped him develop an understanding of how to be a good senior civil servant. Alan embraced the values of some of his bosses and observed which leaders added most value through their interventions and who wasted other people's time. Alan was conscious that some ministers and senior officials managed their vitality far better than others. Alan allowed himself to be shaped by these early experiences, which provided an invaluable framework as he moved into more senior roles.

In practice

- What is the explicit and implicit framework in your mind about what constitutes a good leader?

- How might you apply a framework of vision, values, value-added and vitality to your own leadership role?

- How best do you ensure that the way you apply your leadership framework continues to evolve in the light of experience?

---

1 See *The Four Vs of Leadership: vision, values, value-added and vitality*. Chichester: Capstone.

RECOGNISE THE STRENGTH OF YOUR BELIEFS

THE MORE WE UNDERSTAND the strength of our beliefs, the more we can appreciate the motivation they give us and the risks they can bring.

The idea

Each of us has deep-rooted beliefs about what is important and how best to bring about change. We may believe that it is right to trust people until trust is broken. We may believe that it is right to always give people second and third opportunities and forgive them when they let us down. In contrast, we may have an inner belief that once someone has let us down once, they cannot be trusted again.

An inner belief that out of every problem there will be an opportunity can help carry us through difficult phases. The belief that people always have the potential for good in them can enable us to handle constructively the most challenging of conversations with people we find difficult and demanding.

Strongly held religious and cultural beliefs frame the way we think and lead in subconscious ways. If our world view holds that there are continuing conflicts between good and evil, this will shape the way we view what is happening in organisations where we are a leader. If our frame of reference is that there is always the opportunity for resurrection, with our role being to nurture and grow new life, then we are likely to be focused on drawing out the best in people and able to see the prospect of new life and energy when others do not see this possibility. The risk is we become an inveterate optimist with a potential streak of naivety when observing the motivation and behaviours of others. It can be helpful to share with colleagues the beliefs that flow from our religious and cultural background so that they understand our behaviours and know the strengths and risks that are consequences of our beliefs and convictions.

Alan held in his mind the picture of the seed needing to die before there could be a fruitful harvest. He believed that new life could come out of any situation. The belief that the seed has to die helped Alan recognise that leading change required fundamental shifts, which would be painful. Alan's belief that there was always the prospect of new life meant he was an encourager and supporter to those going through difficult periods. The risk for Alan was in being too much of an optimist and believing that people would always learn constructive lessons from difficult experiences. He had to learn that many people gave up more quickly than he had expected and were more reluctant to believe that there could be a positive outcome.

In practice

- Be clear to yourself what are the underlying cultural and religious beliefs that infuse your thinking.

- See these beliefs as a core part of your inner being that provides you with strength to handle difficult situations.

- Recognise that these beliefs will shape your reaction to situations in ways that could lead to a blinkered approach.

UNDERSTAND WHAT IS SUCCESS FOR YOU

BEING CLEAR WHAT SUCCESS means in every aspect of our lives helps ensure a coherence in the decisions we make and our use of time and energy.

The idea

Success can mean different things at different stages of life. Success in your twenties might be about finding a job or a flat. In your thirties it might be about progressing in your chosen career. In your forties it might be about leading teams well. In your fifties it might be about balancing a range of responsibilities. In your sixties it might be about using those golden years to best effect through influencing and steering others.

Success across the whole of life depends on retaining a balance about what is important to you, including family, community, culture, faith and work. Leading well is likely to involve a willingness to seek success, and if it comes, carrying it lightly. It will require taking responsibility and not running away from accountability. A healthy view of success involves encouraging others to be successful and seeing your mentoring of them as part of your own success. Flexibility is important so that you can move on if success does not come, or if success begins to erode. Despite your best efforts, the success you seek does not always happen, but out of failure or frustration often comes the best learning.

Building success requires commitment, energy and an open mind. It involves listening to others and distilling their perspectives and advice. Building success involves shaping ideas, testing boundaries, building alliances and learning what works and what does not work well.

- Carrying success lightly involves handling setbacks with care and recognising your emotional reactions to setbacks. It includes addressing what might hold you back and discovering ways of building confidence, while seeking to build experience, address frustrations and minimise the fear of failure.

- Building success involves creating forward momentum that anticipates twists and turns and keeps something in reserve.

- Sustaining success is about recognising what you can and cannot control in the future. It is important to be aware of the blinkers that might limit your thinking and be ready to be surprised about opportunities that might open up.[2]

Alan recognised that sometimes his success was a consequence of being in the right place at the right time. On a couple of occasions he had strong sponsorship, which meant he took on leadership responsibilities much earlier than he might otherwise have done: he was thankful for this early experience in exposed leadership positions. On other occasions restructuring exercises meant that his job disappeared. When this happened, the frustration of losing his job was replaced over time by a thankfulness that events had forced decisions that had turned out to have much better outcomes than he could have anticipated. He recognised that sometimes success comes through unexpected events that bring out new qualities and new opportunities.

In practice

- Do not be embarrassed about seeking success; but when it comes, hold it lightly.

- See success as a means of opening up opportunities to create a better future for others.

- Have a holistic view about what success means across every aspect of your life.

- Enable others to develop a definition of success that works for them and integrates their personal values and leadership aspirations.

---

2 See 100 *Great Building Success Ideas*. Singapore: Marshall Cavendish.

KNOW HOW TO WORK EFFECTIVELY WITH OTHERS

THE MORE WE UNDERSTAND how we work effectively with others the better we can apply our leadership gifts to best effect.

The idea

When a team is working well, productivity is high, individual competences and differences are recognised, successes are celebrated and shared. When mistakes happen they are viewed as times of learning and not failure. We have all had the experience of working with people who stimulate creativity. Working jointly with such colleagues can mean the end result is more productive than we had ever expected. There are people we enjoy engaging with where the stimulus of debate challenges our thinking and helps us move on to conclusions we had not previously thought possible.

There are people who frustrate us who we perhaps avoid or are unwilling to share our hopes and hesitations with. The chemistry feels wrong or the preferred approaches are so different that we feel uncomfortable and unwilling to engage in an open-ended and potentially vulnerable way. Those who lead well engage effectively with a wide range of people in a range of different contexts. The more we build up experience of working in different combinations and different teams, the greater will be our understanding of what works or does not work well for us. Participating in a mix of different working environments enables us to develop both formal and informal ways of influencing others and finding outcomes that have the support of a diverse mix of interests.

If you do not have a natural rapport with a particular colleague, it could be a valuable part of your development to do a project jointly with that individual, so that you understand how to bring the best out of someone who has a very different set of preferences to you. You can draw on each other's qualities so that together you are 'more than the sum of the parts'. Working effectively with others is about unleashing the potential in them and letting them have the credit when progress is made. You will be building goodwill with colleagues, which increases their readiness to join with you on shared endeavours. What is most important is that progress is achieved.[3]

The most effective team that Alan was a part of was the executive board of a government department, which included people from a wide range of backgrounds with very different personalities and preferences. They built an understanding of each other and knew how to bring the best out of each other, whether they were working as a full board or in groups of two or three. What made the executive team work well was a deep respect for each other, combined with an enjoyment of each other's company. They were not afraid to be frank with each other when difficult messages needed to be given.

In practice

- How deliberately do you adapt your approach in order to bring the best out in others?

- How might you keep widening your repertoire so that you work effectively with a growing range of people?

- Who do you currently work less effectively with and how might you build a stronger sense of teamwork with that person?

---

3   See 100 *Great Team Effectiveness Ideas*. Singapore: Marshall Cavendish.

APPRECIATE WHAT GIVES YOU DAILY FULFILMENT

A COMBINATION OF LONG-TERM commitment and belief, alongside daily fulfilment, helps keep up the energy to lead consistently well.

The idea

Physically and emotionally we need to be sustained on a daily basis. We need an underlying sense of purpose if we are to be spiritually fulfilled.

Just as we need to eat each day to sustain us physically, we need to be sustained emotionally, intellectually and spiritually on a daily basis. If someone is going through a difficult period as a leader I would often suggest that they note down at the end of each day three things that have gone well. At the end of each week they might write down three insights they have learned from their experiences that week. The more somebody can identify where they have made a difference or contribution, the more they can feel fulfilled and affirmed.

Some organisations have a very strong culture of celebration and affirming staff, even when things go wrong. It is tough if your team fails to win a tender, but if there are genuine, appreciative comments about the effort your team put in, you can then move on more purposefully.

Fulfilment comes through standing back and seeing the journey you have travelled, and being able to smile at what has flowed less easily than you would have liked. It can be helpful to keep some symbols of progress, such as some appreciative letters or a pen or book that dated from a particular era or event. Having moments of giving thanks recognises the rhythms that work for us as human beings. Enjoy them and do not resist embracing them.

Alan recognised the importance of daily rituals. The 15 minute walk into St James' Park in central London helped refresh his mind on busy days. Alan recognised that he needed to break up the routine of the day so there was a fulfilment from different activities, wherever this was possible. An evening routine of hot blackcurrant cordial followed by a hot bath were rituals that relaxed him and gave him a sense of calm.

In practice

- Recognise the types of fulfilment that keep you fresh and alert.

- Remember the importance of celebrating progress, however small, and do not regard celebration as indulgence.

- Remember to give thanks daily for the gifts and opportunities you have been given.

- Recognise the routines that relax and calm you and seek to build them into the day.

DITCH OUT-OF-DATE REASONS FOR YOUR ACTIONS

We can be captive to habitual ways of doing things and need to be open to developing a different rationale and self-belief.

The idea

The reasons for our actions might be because we have always done things in a particular way. We have inherited or adopted an approach that has worked well in the past and has provided a rationale for the way we do things. We may believe there is one way of doing things and one right or wrong answer to a question. We might be captive to a particular description of success that we need to update.

When I work with a leader starting a new role I invite them to think through what is needed in this new context and what good leadership would therefore look like. The key starting point is what does the context demand, rather than just applying actions that have been used before into this new context. The fact that we have done something before in a way that has worked well does not mean it is the right thing to do in a new context.

The consequence of rapidly changing information technology means that we need to be continually thinking about how to lead and communicate in a fast-moving, globally-connected world. We need to identify the outcomes we are moving towards, the attitude of mind we need to embrace, and the actions that are most important to ensure those outcomes happen. We cannot rely on assumptions about what has worked well in the past. We need to embrace the delight of exploring new and different ways of building engagement, partnership and shared agendas.

Alan had been bought up to think that government ministers were able to weigh up arguments in an objective way and reach conclusions that would be the most effective way forward. The ideal submission would provide the minister with the information and options they needed to reach the ideal answer. Alan rapidly learnt that decision-making was not as straightforward. The government minister was weighing up emotional reactions as well as facts. They needed to talk issues through rather than just address them on paper. They needed to be encouraged to think through how different people would react and, therefore, identify unintended consequences of what might seem eminently sensible decisions. Alan learnt to recognise that the quality of dialogue he could establish with a government minister was even more important than the quality of any written submission.

In practice

- Recognise if you are adopting ways of thinking and acting that do not quite resonate with others.

- Observe how others reach an agreed outcome with their bosses or key interlocutors, and reflect on how you might be able to engage more effectively as a consequence of this learning.

- Keep refreshing your repertoire of approaches for getting things done and influencing others.

RECOGNISE WHEN YOU NEED TO MOVE ON FROM SOMEONE ELSE'S BELIEFS

WE LEARN A LOT through embracing the leadership of others, but there is a point when we need to move on and be authentic in bringing our own approach to leading well.

The idea

When you work for a leader you admire, you soak up a lot of their approach, which influences the way you approach your own leadership challenges. We readily adopt frameworks that have worked well for others and make them our own. Their effectiveness gives us the confidence to use approaches that might not come easily to us. There is a risk that we can become a clone of a successful leader and do not develop the full range of leadership approaches that we have the potential to develop.

When I am coaching leaders applying for more senior roles, I invite them to think about what they admire about people who have done similar jobs and in what ways they embrace attitudes and approaches their exemplars display. I also encourage them to think through what they authentically bring to leadership and how it is different to those they admire. I seek to draw out the distinctiveness of an individual's background and experience and how that feeds into a style of leadership that is personal, individual and not captive to anyone else's legacy or beliefs.

To lead well you have to be comfortable in your own skin, understanding how you deploy your gifts to good effect and integrate the wealth of your experience and insights into a coherent, believable narrative.

Alan held in his mind's eye a leader who inspired him who was always energetic and engaging. This individual had exuberant energy and always offered a stimulating viewpoint across a wide range of different issues. As Alan moved into new leadership roles he initially sought to model himself on this individual's approach, but it was exhausting. Perhaps Alan did not need to get into every subject in quite as much detail. Perhaps what was needed was a different type of leadership who steered and influenced but did not try to be everywhere or seek to have a hundred ideas before breakfast. Alan continued to apply the freshness of thinking and curiosity of his mentor, but deliberately moved away from adopting his hyper-energetic style.

In practice

- Who are the leadership heroes whose approaches you have embraced?

- To what extent are you captive to the leadership approaches of particular role models?

- How best do you articulate your own, clear narrative of good leadership in a way that is unique to you?

RECOGNISE THE SHIFTING PHASES OF LIFE

As you move through life it is helpful to recalibrate what is important to you and how you seek to contribute in different spheres.

The idea

I recently had a conversation with someone who had just reached the age of 60 in which she spoke about her retirement and going back to activities she had done in the past. We talked about reframing her narrative, with her drawing on her breadth of experiences when moving into the next phase of life. This reframing of her narrative helped her to describe her future with a smile on her face. It was not a matter of going back. She was looking forward to enjoying her golden years doing a portfolio of different activities that would enable her to influence internationally, nationally and locally. She was moving from executive leadership into a sequence of non-executive roles where she could advise, influence and mentor.

In different phases of our lives the opportunity to lead evolves. Initially we bring the ability to master details and be on top of a discreet function. We develop the capability to lead a team and then influence a wider cross-section of people. We might graduate to become a member of an executive team or having ultimate responsibility for a particular area. We might then move into advisory roles or non-executive positions where we are steering and mentoring.

It may be that you particularly enjoyed the contribution you made at one stage of life and might want to renew your application of those qualities at a later stage: the context might have changed, as you will be using those qualities differently and probably with different people.

Changes in the economy and society happen whether we like it or not. We either keep up and adapt, or fall behind. We are in a continuous process of recognising the different phases in our individual journey and responding to changes happening around us.

Alan had enjoyed working with government ministers for over 30 years, but there was a repetition in the work that led to his enthusiasm waning. He recognised that the time was right to move into another phase of life, which could be as an executive leader, a consultant or a coach. Alan explored each of these options and began to realise that his enthusiasm for taking on another executive role was less than it might have been a few years previously. He knew he could be excited by consultancy or coaching and approached these two options with a sense of anticipation about the next phase of life.

In practice

- How fixed is your view of leadership? Has your perspective changed over time?

- What do you foresee as the next phase in your contribution as a leader, and what might that be?

- What beliefs about yourself as a leader do you now need to refine?

- How can you use significant birthdays to reframe the leadership approach you want to bring in the next phase of your life?

BE HONEST WITH YOURSELF ABOUT YOUR AMBITIONS

There is no point in holding on to outdated ambitions. We need to keep updating our ambitions in the light of experience and reality.

The idea

There is a time and place to talk about your ambitions. When you are having a performance review with your boss you want the best possible guidance about your development, hence being clear on your ambitions provides a framework for your development. On many occasions being too overt about your ambitions creates antipathy from others and generates a greater sense of competition than is helpful.

For some people their level of ambition is unhelpfully low. An individual may have lots of potential but be holding back on their aspirations. This reluctance has held many people back and meant that the quality of leadership in many organisations has been restricted because those with the greatest potential have often felt a reluctance to develop or show their ambition. Excessive deference or humility has got in the way of them using their abilities and potential to the full.

It can be helpful to have a frank conversation with a coach or mentor about your embryonic ambitions and where you believe you can make a significant impact. It helps to be frank about those ambitions and then talk through how realistic they are and what would need to happen for those ambitions to materialise. Perhaps it is helpful to put together a plan about how you can prepare for and explore these possibilities. It is often helpful to have more than one focus for your ambitions so your sense of fulfilment is not dependent upon one particular avenue opening up.

Core to your ambition might be a strong sense of service where personal achievement is irrelevant. The ambition may be focused on young people you might enthuse, or older people whose lives could be made better because of your interventions. Be willing to be ambitious about what might be possible and seek to make a difference. Do not let a false sense of inadequacy or humility stop you from aspiring to make the impact you believe is right.

In his early career, Alan had been ambitious to demonstrate that a Yorkshire lad could reach senior levels in government service. He was willing to take on tough jobs and work in a determined way to ensure progress. His sense of ambition evolved as he spent an increasing amount of time mentoring and coaching his staff. A new sense of ambition developed that was about enabling others to step up effectively to take on demanding leadership challenges.

In practice

- See a strong sense of ambition as helpful.

- Do not be too blinkered in your ambitions and allow them to expand over time.

- Be open about your ambitions with those you trust who can give you good advice.

- Take your ambitions seriously, and at the same time embrace them with a light touch.

SECTION B
WHAT?

WAKE UP AND DREAM

WHEN WE WAKE UP and dream we open our thinking to different possibilities for the future.

The idea

It might be time to wake up and dream. There are barriers to be addressed and potential opportunities to take forward. It could be time to look more widely and dream about what might be possible. Now could be the moment to be open to different avenues and be excited about the difference you can make.

The apparent contradiction between 'wake up' and 'dream' is deliberate. Waking up to new realities is a precursor to dreaming in an open and fruitful way. There are moments when we need to combine realism with a sense of adventure. Following one's imagination can transform the aspirations of individuals, groups and teams. It can give confidence to think big, entertain new possibilities and turn hopes into practical next steps.

Waking up to the future requires accepting the realities of the past and present, while not being overwhelmed by them. Waking up to the next phase of life is about being ready to dream, bringing an open mind and recognising that you have competencies and insights that will be valuable for new situations.

Dreaming well is not about moving into a land of unreal fantasy. Dreaming well is about bringing creativity, being open to the unexpected, being willing to step into the unknown with a sense of anticipation, and allowing yourself to believe that you can make a contribution that is more significant than you had previously anticipated.

There might be a moment when you wake up to your dreams and begin to discern what could be possible. There may be times when you are dreaming through darkness, when you have to handle dreams with care. Following your dreams can take you into new and worthwhile places that you had not previously anticipated. A dream might be about moving into a new leadership role, building a wider influence in a portfolio of activities, or balancing your personal and work responsibilities more effectively. Dreaming from pillow to pathway involves allowing a dream to develop in your mind and then turning it into practical propositions and next steps.[4]

Jeanette was head of year at a secondary school. She enjoyed her responsibilities, but sometimes became frustrated by the decisions of the leadership team. Jeanette's colleague, Henry, suggested that the best way that she could solve these problems was by becoming a member of the senior team. Henry encouraged her to think about what type of member she would be. Jeanette was taken aback by this suggestion and was challenged to think through whether she wanted to be one of the school leaders or not. Initially she was hesitant, but then recognised that she had much to offer.

In practice

- What type of dreams do you have about your future?

- What are the realities you need to wake up to?

- How best can you turn your dreams about the future into reality?

- With whom can you test whether your dreams might be realistic?

- How can you accept that your dreams might have substance and not just be a figment of your imagination?

---

4 See *Wake Up and Dream: stepping into your future*. Norwich: Canterbury Press.

LOOK FOR THE SILVER LINING

WHENEVER LIFE IS GOING less well keep looking for the silver lining.

The idea

When you are in a busy job there is a risk that you can get worn down by what is going wrong. You believe it is important to keep a forward momentum going. You quickly move on from what has gone well and want to address the next issue, but when something does not work well you can become preoccupied and stuck. In your mind a partial success turns into an embarrassing failure. Instead of celebrating your good progress, you can become mired in self-reflection and be at risk of wallowing in anxiety about what has gone less well and potential worst-case consequences.

When something goes less well it is always worth posing the question: 'What is the silver lining?' When progress is bumpier, there might be a greater readiness to be open to a modified approach. The silver lining could be suggesting change and a willingness of others to listen more readily to your suggestions.

Where resources have become tighter in hospitals, the silver lining has sometimes been a willingness to look at the way things are done to see what greater efficiencies and effectiveness can be delivered, rather than expecting ever-growing financial resources.

Regularly asking yourself, 'Where is the silver lining?' helps to keep you positive and optimistic, whatever is happening around you. There is always hope for the future. It is worth having a mindset that there will always be 'light at the end of the tunnel'.

Jeanette was dismayed that the exam results were not improving as much as she had hoped. She was disappointed for the pupils and her colleagues, but the silver lining was likely to be that her colleagues would be more open to changes in the way the curriculum was organised. In some subjects teaching methods needed to be looked at afresh: there was likely to be a greater willingness to do some practical in-service development. Jeanette could see opportunities opening up for her ideas to be considered.

In practice

- Accept that dark clouds bring fruitful rain.

- Always look for the opportunities that might flow from disappointments.

- Be willing to be positive and optimistic in searching for opportunities in even the darkest of circumstances.

- Embrace the belief that there is always a silver lining to keep you measured and cheerful.

KEEP PRACTISING AND REHEARSING

THE BEST LEADERS NEVER stop practising their skills or rehearsing their contribution.

The idea

Rehearsal is different from practice and from performance. This is as true for leaders of organisations as for musicians: we can perform better with good preparation and can always learn from how musicians prepare to perform. Practice helps musicians learn new skills that keep them up to the mark. Whereas practice is solitary work on technique, rehearsal involves collective improvement: it is the work the team does in order to be ready to perform for an audience.

Martin Elliott is Medical Director at Great Ormond Street Hospital and one of the world's leading paediatric cardiothoracic surgeons. He is a musician and brings to life his presentations on leadership and improvement in surgical teams by showing how they have learned from other high-performing teams whose work demands speed, accuracy and coordination (for example, Formula 1 racing teams and the Red Arrows aerobatic display team). He sums up much of this learning in a single phrase: rehearse, rehearse and rehearse.

What can teams learn from what musicians do in rehearsal? Listening is as important as playing. By listening in rehearsal musicians develop relationships among their parts about who will take the lead and who will follow. Not all orchestral coordination comes from the tip of a conductor's baton. Ensemble emerges from the understanding that musicians develop in rehearsal how their parts interact with the whole orchestra.

For all leaders, watching and listening is as important as what is said and done. In preparing teams to perform well leaders are not simply issuing instructions; they are helping team members find how best to fit their contributions to each other. Most musicians come to rehearsal already knowing the notes and will have played the piece many times before. They use rehearsals to develop a shared vision of how they want the music to sound, what impression they want to leave, and what feelings they want to evoke. Time spent individually practicing and then rehearsing as a team improves both quality and creative interaction, which together leads to outstanding performance.[5]

Jeanette was conscious that she could speak spontaneously in a way that inspired and entertained. She recognised that she needed to refine this skill so that she could adapt it to the groups she was addressing, be they colleagues, parents or pupils. Preparing and rehearsing did not come naturally to her but she recognised that she needed to work closely with her colleagues so that together they improved on the quality of the curricular submissions and in the way they coordinated activities across the school.

In practice

- What parallels are relevant between the way musicians practice and rehearse and the way you as a leader need to practice and rehearse?

- What skills do you need to practice to become even better at them?

- What do you need to rehearse with colleagues so that the combined impact is consistently impressive?

- How readily do you create the time and motivation for practice and rehearsal?

---

5   See *Knowing the Score.* London: Praesta (co-authored with Ken Thomson).

14   HOLD YOUR NERVE

THERE ARE MOMENTS WHEN you need to go through a pain barrier and keep going, whatever frustration or discomfort you experience.

The idea

Just before writing this chapter I watched Alistair Brownlee win the 2016 Olympic triathlon gold medal. He had to hold his nerve during the swimming and the tough climbs and descents of the cycling leg. Alistair kept running hard in the marathon stage through excruciating pain to win the Olympic gold in a convincing manner. He had trained himself to keep focused, live with the pain and continue regardless, fixed on his goal.

There are times for any leader when it is painful. You are pushing yourself hard to reach outcomes. You may have to fend off criticism, with people questioning your direction or even competence. You may be having painful conversations and giving difficult messages. You may have to work within a tough financial regime. It can feel relentless as you handle consistently difficult issues. You have to hold your nerve and focus on the outcomes you want to deliver.

What might help you hold your nerve is a belief that you are doing the right thing, a focus on the difference you are seeking to make, and the assurance that you have the support of key people in your life—together with the encouragement from those who believe in you and what you are seeking to do. Holding your nerve involves recognising the pain, remembering how you have handled it before, believing that you can move through a pain barrier, and believing that there will be respite in due course.

Holding your nerve does involve looking after yourself. Alistair Brownlee was drinking water at regular intervals. He was pacing himself so he could complete the course. In the cycle leg he was working cooperatively with other cyclists. All these parallels apply to how we hold our nerve and use our physical and emotional resources to best effect in leadership roles.

Jeanette knew that it would take time to persuade her colleagues that the curriculum planning exercise was necessary. She had to handle some dismissive comments that everyone was too busy and tired. She was persistent in a positive and encouraging way. Jeanette ensured that an in-service training day was allocated for this review. She ensured there was effective preparation for this day and kept up the momentum to ensure outcomes were reached, however sceptical her colleagues might have been at the start.

In practice

- What helps you move through pain barriers?

- How best do you hold your nerve when others around you are sceptical or critical?

- What practical next steps might you take to cope with criticism and scepticism?

- Are there situations where you need to hold your nerve today and how are you going to do this?

15

KEEP AGILE

INDIVIDUALS AND TEAMS NEED to embed competencies and attitudes that produce confident, surefooted agility when needed.

The idea

Agility is the facility to act and react fast and decisively, and to move into and out of situations with surefooted confidence, in order to exploit opportunities and avoid potential threats. Agility requires mental alertness that informs, and is informed by, a high state of suppleness and fitness. It is a state of readiness and of being, albeit one that needs to be rested to conserve energy and strength for when they are most needed. It is important to develop agility for when you need it. Once the time has come, if you and your organisation do not possess agility it is too late to start working on it.

Agility is not restless, aimless action. It is not purposeful action at the wrong time. It is rarely a heavy-change management programme. Agility is about travelling light in the correct general direction with strategic goals held carefully in mind.

An agile leader sustains momentum, has adult conversations, encourages initiatives and frames the content for others. The effective, agile leader recognises they have choices and exercises those choices well. The agile leader listens to the small voice within, allowing the subconscious to make connections that are hard to articulate. The agile team is focused on where it can make the biggest difference. It is integrating with the informal organisation and avoiding isolation.

The agile organisation is comprehending its environment, carefully achieving and maintaining organisational resilience, and ensuring that stakeholders continue to be fully engaged and understood. The agile organisation is continuing to develop its organisational capability and always seeking to get onto the front foot. The individual leader needs to maintain agility in order to respond in a timely way to changing circumstances. Agility is not an optional extra. It is a prerequisite of long-term success.[6]

Jeanette was inspired watching the Olympic cycling from the Rio de Janeiro velodrome. The cyclists were exemplars of fitness, endurance and teamwork. They navigated situations where they were bunched together without fear of crashing. There was a clarity of intent to cycle fast and a recognition that they were often working in tandem with each other. Jeanette drew from examples of agility in cycling when talking with her colleagues about how they could bring the best out of each other.

In practice

- What enables you to act and react fast when needed?

- How best do you maintain your mental alertness when the pace is fast-moving?

- How can you be both focused on outcomes that are important and agile in the moment?

- How best do you ensure you do not waste your energy at the wrong time on the wrong issue?

---

6 See *The Age of Agility*. London: Praesta (co-authored with Steve Wigzell).

BE WILLING TO TAKE A BIG LEAP

16

SOMETIMES THERE IS THE scope and a need for a big leap forward. Be ready to take that opportunity.

The idea

The way we develop as leaders is rarely in a straight line. There are moments when we have to make a significant step up. This might flow from promotion or from the need for us to fill a gap. Athletes who train together are continually stretching each other so that everyone's performance is raised. In the best of leadership teams there is a mutual support and challenge that enables each individual to keep growing in their resolve and effectiveness.

Raising your game starts with understanding your strengths and your less strong points, embedding your values and creating a sustainable equilibrium between different areas of your life. Raising your game on a sustainable basis involves addressing your self-doubts and fears, and believing you can do difficult things well. It greatly helps if you have supporters and stakeholders who are sources of practical encouragement. As you up the pace you will be developing your skills in influencing others and converting your critics, as well as understanding how best to respond to problems. Essential to raising your game will be keeping your focus, growing your resilience and renewing your freshness.

To take a big leap requires an inner confidence and conviction that you have a worthwhile contribution to make. A sense of vocation or purpose can underpin the resolve that is needed to be consistently focused on delivering outcomes over an extended period. It is one thing to raise your game for a ten minute burst of activity, while it is in a different league to raise your game to lead your part of an organisation consistently well; hence the importance of good preparation, holding your nerve and keeping agile.[7]

Jeanette knew that if she wanted to become a candidate for a senior post at the school she would have to raise her game. She needed to move from being a critic to being a positive mover and shaker within the staffroom. Jeanette needed to demonstrate that she could see the bigger picture and be able to steer people consistently in a direction so there was an alignment of aspiration and endeavour. Jeannette recognised that she needed to lead from the front rather than prod from behind.

In practice

- Switch your mindset into believing that you can do difficult things and convert your critics.

- Understand in what way you have raised your game over the last year and what enabled you to do that.

- Be explicit about how you need to raise your game in the next phase.

- Be conscious of where you need to switch your approach from prodding from behind to leading from the front.

- Recognise that you will need to hold your self-doubt in check.

---

7 See *Raise Your Game: how to succeed at work*. Chichester: Capstone.

KEEP EXTENDING YOUR COMFORT ZONE

It can help to deliberately keep extending your comfort zone with particular tasks or responsibilities you find difficult.

The idea

You will be conscious that you feel perfectly comfortable doing some activities while other activities require much more mental and emotional energy. Our energy levels can be sapped if we are continually having to lead on activities that drain us.

For example, if chairing a meeting is exhausting the last thing you may want to do is volunteer to chair meetings, but if you volunteer to chair smaller and less important meetings it can build up your competency and confidence. You may be hesitant about speaking in front of large gatherings. One approach is to volunteer to speak at small and relatively less important events, such as a local community meeting.

Extending your comfort zone might be about developing techniques and building up experience. It might also be about developing a mindset that certain activities, which you thought were impossible, are doable. What is key is seeking to reduce the anxiety levels linked with particular activities so that you can take on such activities with a greater degree of equanimity.

Clearly identify those areas where you want to extend your comfort zone and then deliberately push the boundaries of your practice and experience in those areas. Do not be too ambitious initially, or your anxieties could increase rather than reduce, but be deliberate and measured, then acknowledge your progress to yourself and others.

Jeanette thought of herself as a doer rather than a thinker. She was at her best in dealing with day-to-day, practical issues. Jeanette recognised she needed to develop greater confidence in dealing with long-term issues. She volunteered to take on a piece of work about the pastoral arrangements in the school, which required her to think about what they needed to have in place in two years' time. Jeanette forced herself to practice thinking and planning on a longer-term basis.

In practice

- Be honest with yourself about which activities are in your comfort zone and which are outside that zone.

- Recognise how you have previously extended your comfort zone.

- Be explicit about a couple of areas where you want to become more competent and relaxed in the way you lead.

- Decide where you can experiment in a relatively safe place.

- Celebrate your progress and clearly recognise where you have extended your comfort zone.

NAVIGATE CAREFULLY THROUGH TURBULENT TIMES

Be ready for turbulent times and never waste a crisis.

The idea

Strong leaders maintain their core attitudes and beliefs through turbulent times, no matter how much pressure they come under. This involves being clear what you think is the right thing to do whilst being honest about how the turbulence is affecting you. It includes recognising when you may be about to 'lose it' and stepping away to take a break from the situation, however briefly.

Working effectively through turbulence involves tackling each new challenge clearly and calmly, leading from the front to inspire those around you. It includes keeping a sense of perspective where you seek the best information you can, listen carefully to the views of others and have personal sounding boards. Throughout the turbulence, creating a personal space where you can think clearly is critical. As you tackle each new challenge, setting clear priorities, drawing on the right team and being visible as a leader will reinforce your ability to hold your nerve and take people with you.

During times of uncertainty and turbulence there is a clear need for visible, personal leadership so that people are as informed as possible, with you setting the tone about how you expect the organisation to behave. During extreme uncertainty, it is unlikely you will have many answers to people's questions, but silence breeds rumour and negative energy. People need information to be able to understand where to focus and prioritise. It is vital to communicate constantly to keep the dialogue open. People will look for any signals that you feel things are out of control. The perception of your mood will spread quickly and will often become distorted through gossip.

Living through turbulence requires you to look after yourself in a planned and careful way. It involves building stamina that fuels creative and mental energy, as well as finding a state of equilibrium that helps you remain calm and balanced. It might well involve engaging your mind in something different from everyday work, no matter how trivial, as a source of release and to stimulate creativity. Continually returning to what matters most in your life will help keep things in perspective, whether it comes from enduring interests or relationships, or is rooted in beliefs and faith.[8]

Jeanette was initially shocked by a negative external assessment of the school's performance. There was inevitably a period of turbulence while the highlighted issues were addressed. Jeanette recognised that she needed to keep a cool head and a sense of perspective. She knew that certain things needed to change. She focused on the changes that she thought were right while keeping a positive mindset about the viability of the desired outcomes. During this busy period she was deliberate in looking after herself and sought to avoid getting overstressed.

In practice

- See turbulence as potentially a creative period.
- Be clear what are the core attitudes and beliefs that you need to maintain.
- Be focused about the individual challenges you face and tackle each of them clearly and calmly.
- Be deliberate in looking after yourself and maintaining stamina and well-being.

---

8 See *Riding the Rapids*. London: Praesta (co-authored with Jane Stephens).

UNDERSTAND YOUR ACCOUNTABILITIES

BEING CLEAR ABOUT THE definition of your accountabilities will help you focus your efforts and reduce energy wasted worrying about things that are not within your control.

The idea

Whenever you start a new role, or when a role is reshaped, it is important to be clear what are your accountabilities. Sometimes accountabilities can accrete: it is worth reviewing them and agreeing what they currently are so that ambiguity and uncertainty is reduced.

Accountability is not the same as responsibility. You will be allocating responsibilities to members of your staff. You may set a clear expectation that an individual delivers a report by a particular date. You set clear guidelines for what goes into the report and you retain accountability for the overall direction and quality of what is delivered. You do not need to feel accountable for every sentence in the report: that is the responsibility of the team member in the lead. Your accountability is at the quality assurance level.

Understanding your accountabilities is both about overall performance, the quality of what is done (and how it is done under your watch), and about the steering you give your staff. They need to feel that they have full responsibility for the actions they take.

Sometimes you might feel that you have a personal accountability for progress when it is a matter for the team as a whole and is a corporate responsibility. I observe quite a lot of leaders with an over-developed sense of their personal responsibility. The consequence can be that they take too much onto their shoulders and seek to solve problems themselves rather than being explicit about their expectations of others.

Jeanette knew she had a tendency to want to solve everyone's problems. If she was going to progress in her career she needed to recognise the difference between carrying ultimate accountability and being clear where individual responsibility lay. When planning the curriculum with colleagues she became more disciplined at agreeing what she was going to do and what was the expectation on others. She did not shirk from her overall accountability but became more disciplined at clarifying where an individual's responsibilities lay.

In practice

- Clarify to yourself the difference between overall accountability and individual responsibility.

- Be explicit about the accountably you hold.

- Beware lest your accountabilities keep growing exponentially, especially when there is limited clarity about who is individually responsible for particular activities.

- Be mindful if you have an over-developed sense of responsibility that results in you wanting to solve everyone else's problems for them.

20 DEVELOP YOUR IMPACT

OUR PERSONAL IMPACT FLOWS from clarity about who we are, what we stand for, where we place our priorities, when we choose to act, and understanding why we respond in a particular way.

The idea

Personal impact stems from getting the tone and timing right. The strength of an argument is only one consideration. What matters is that you pitch the tone right so that others believe your arguments and are open to be persuaded by them. Timing is important, as you want your views to be expressed when others are most likely to be responsive. Personal impact is occasionally about forcefulness, but more often it is about focus and the fine-tuning of arguments to fit particular contexts. Personal impact often flows from patience and persistence.

Crucial to personal impact is knowing ourselves and our preference well, knowing how we contribute effectively, and knowing what our end goals are. Personal impact is inevitably about delivering outcomes. A key starting point is identifying the outcome you want to achieve after realistic assessment of what is possible.

What matters most is making choices about the tone you want to set. Those people I have worked with who have had the biggest personal impact have had clarity about what they are aiming for, conviction about the values that are most important to them, and the courage to act where necessary. This is accompanied by an attitude towards others that is courteous and caring. Their personal impact has come from exercising both a toughness and a warmth in relation to both themselves and others.

Developing your personal impact can be an enjoyable exploration as you build on your strengths, try different approaches, develop adaptability, crystallize learning and enjoy all the interactions that flow from working across a range of different situations. Key to developing your personal impact is preparing well, deliberately varying your approach, and demonstrating that you listen and understand. It involves ensuring you assess likely reactions, keep communicating and build a shared clarity about expectations. It involves knowing your priorities, the relative strength of your position and who your allies are.[9]

Jeanette recognised that she needed to focus her personal impact, as she could give the impression of having a scattergun approach. She recognised that she needed to plan ahead more carefully and recognised the concerns of some of her colleagues. She wanted to find a win/win outcome more readily. She recognised that building relationships would create a situation where her colleagues would be more likely to accept her preferred approach. She needed to ensure she did not look and sound negative when they expressed reservations. Jeanette observed that the more positive she was the more likely it would be that her colleagues would accept her preferred approach.

In practice

- When has your impact been at its greatest and why?

- How best do you clarify the areas where you want to have the biggest impact?

- Where does effective preparation affect the way you seek to influence others?

- How might you vary your style and approach to take account of individual people and situations more effectively?

---

9 See *100 Great Personal Impact Ideas*. Singapore: Marshall Cavendish.

SECTION C
WHO?

CULTIVATE YOUR CHAMPIONS

Recognise the importance of champions and sponsors and acknowledge their contribution.

The idea

A professional football team will use experienced former footballers to look for talent and then nurture that talent. The 17-year-old footballer with talent will gain hugely from a champion who believes in him, encourages him and helps him recognise both his potential and the hard work needed to attain that potential.

During the first ten years of my career in government I can recall three people (Hugh Jenkins, Nick Monck and Jim Hamilton) who believed in me and helped me stretch my thinking about what was possible. I was also conscious that they were my champions when it came to discussions about performance and next steps.

Cultivating your champions is not about ingratiating yourself to them or about flattering them. It is about demonstrating continuous and conspicuous competence and effectiveness. Your champions will know that your commitment is rock solid and that you will not let other people down. They will only want to advocate your credentials if they have complete trust in the values that drive you and the motivation that underpins your commitment.

When someone has been your champion and you have moved to another area of work it is important to keep in touch. There might be ongoing opportunities to contribute to pieces of work they are leading on. At some point you will need people to speak up about you and write references on your behalf.

When someone has been your champion at one stage of your career, do not forget them if you move on to greater things. Where you owe a debt of gratitude to someone, don't forget them: periodically thank them for their help, even though their role as your champion may be long gone.

Jo had successfully completed training on the National Health Service Graduate Scheme. She was now in her third leadership role, and was benefiting from the advice of an experienced manager. There were moments when she was frustrated by the amount of advice but recognised that this manager would be an important person to cultivate and learn from. As her career progressed Jo would need champions who would speak up for her and write positive references when she wanted to move on, hence her acceptance that cultivating this manager was a worthwhile investment for the longer term.

In practice

- Who has been a champion of yours in the past and why did that happen?

- Who are your potential champions now and how best do you invest in those relationships?

- Who do you need to thank who has been your champion in the past, even though the two of you are now in very different spheres?

- Who would you ask to write a reference for you and how best do you keep in contact with them and keep them up-to-date with your progress?

RECOGNISE THOSE WHO CARE ABOUT YOU

22

HOWEVER AMBITIOUS OR COMMITTED you are to your work, always remember to look after the needs of those who care for you.

The idea

When your work is demanding your work commitments can dominate and stop you from appreciating the needs of those who care about you the most. An overriding sense of vocation or ambition can be destructive to family or personal relationships. Where progress in your work involves moving from place to place, the consequences for family life can be harmful over the longer term. Some who moved often geographically when they were children remember the experience as a positive one that has shaped their character. For others, movement from place to place detrimentally affected their confidence and left them with anxieties that they still find difficult to handle.

A few decades ago there was a general acceptance that one person's career in a family came first. Now there is much more of an expectation that both partners will pursue careers. The big positive from this cultural shift is the acceptance that the preferences of both people in a partnership have to be taken into account, with equal attention given to each other's future work activities.

As your career progresses, don't forget your parents. They will have committed time, energy and resources for the first 20 years of your life to enable you to get started in your working life. By updating them on what you are doing and reflecting on your learning from them, you will be giving your parents immense pleasure and pride.

Allowing them to share in the ups and downs of your working life will give them lasting joy in the latter years of their life.

It is well worth creating and celebrating milestones with those who care about you. For example, I treasure the memory of the rowing trip my daughter organised for our family to celebrate the sixty-seventh birthday of Frances and me.

Jo was glad to be promoted and was focused on her next steps. She had not appreciated how delighted her parents would be: for them her promotions from the graduate scheme to successive leadership posts were major milestones. It was the fulfilment of the efforts and energy they had put into parenting Jo. This recognition reminded Jo that on future occasions, when there were milestones in her career, that she needed to celebrate with her parents and allow them the pleasure of enjoying her progress to the full.

In practice

- Be mindful if you are subjugating the needs of those who care for you to your professional needs over a long period.

- Think through what type of recognition is particularly appreciated by those who care for you.

- Do not allow your sense of independence to rebuff those who care for you.

SHARE YOUR JOURNEY

BUILDING UP COMPANIONS ON the way will help provide mutual support and courage.

The idea

As you face a succession of leadership challenges you can often feel isolated and alone. You may feel that those who work for you are hesitant about expressing frustrations or problems. The more senior you become the more valuable are conversations with others on similar or parallel journeys to you.

I have coached various participants on high-potential development schemes within the UK Government. One of the benefits of these schemes was the building up of mutual respect between peers from different government departments. In their day jobs they did not have much cause to be in contact with each other, but being part of a development scheme required them to work together on shared projects and in different learning sets. They developed a strong sense of mutual support, which in many cases continued over subsequent years.

When I lead workshops I encourage people to think about whether there are fellow participants with whom they would like to keep in contact for their mutual benefit. Mutual mentoring conversations, over time, need to be two-way if they are to be of sustainable value to both parties. Deliberately ensuring that there is a broad equality of benefits helps sustain this type of mutual sharing and mentoring.

Sharing your journey involves being willing to talk through your experience with a range of other people so that they benefit from what has worked effectively for you. The more open you are, the more likely it is that others are going to share their parallel experiences with you.

Jo kept in touch through social media with a number of people on the graduate training scheme, and invested most time in two individuals with whom she had had particularly engaging conversations on the training scheme. The three of them agreed to meet up on a periodic basis to share their experiences and stretch each other's thinking about their own next steps. These conversations every three months were central to Jo articulating what she had learnt in handling a range of different work issues.

In practice

- Whose journey has been parallel to yours with whom you can usefully share experiences?

- Who is on a similar journey in a different profession or organisation whose experience you can learn from?

- With whom can you do mutual mentoring that will benefit you both?

- How systematic do you want to be in planning forward conversations with people on similar journeys?

- How best can you acknowledge the contribution of those who are companions on your journey?

BUILD YOUR PERSONAL SUPPORT

HAVING THE RIGHT TYPE of personal support in place is essential for your success and well-being, whatever your place in the overall leadership structure.

The idea

A key factor that makes a significant difference to the life and well-being of a leader is the nature of their personal support. The leader who is worried about how accurate their diary is or whether their IT arrangements are consistently reliable will be using energy that distracts them from delivering what is most important as a leader. It is always worth investing time and resources to ensure your personal support arrangements are robust.

At a junior leadership level this is about having effective IT systems in place and knowing where you can find information without having to worry about its accessibility. It means having a network of colleagues and friends who will encourage and support you when the going gets tough.

At more senior levels personal support might be about someone managing your diary and the flow of e-mails and paper. What matters are clear guidelines to enable those who are providing your personal support to do this in an independent and responsible way, meaning that you do not have to worry about detail being overlooked.

Building your personal support is about recognising who encourages you and helps you be creative. You might want to ensure that you have regular, short conversations with people who make you smile and with whom you feel positive about talking through issues you need to tackle.

When you observe cycle racing you see the strongest competitors supporting each other as they take turns in leading the peloton. This illustrates that even with people with whom you are in competition, it is worth considering the usefulness of mutual support.

Jo had previously managed her own time and diary. As she began to move into more responsible leadership roles she recognised that some of her time was spent on activities that were best done by others. Jo had not previously used the clerical support available to the team. Over time she recognised that if she could rely on others, it would allow her to focus on the difficult issues that were her prime responsibility. She became much less hesitant about drawing on the personal support of both junior staff and her colleagues.

In practice

- What type of personal support might be available to you that you do not currently use?

- What tasks that currently take your time might others do on your behalf?

- How can you balance your own independence of action with using the resources available from others to best effect?

KNOW WHO IS COMMITTED TO YOUR SUCCESS

THOSE WHO ARE COMMITTED to your success will give time to you and offer you the benefit of the doubt for a period.

The idea

When you have been appointed to a new role, those appointing you want you to succeed. They are committed to your success, as they will look foolish if they have made a bad appointment. Because they selected you they will want to encourage and support you over the initial few months. They will be available to give advice and support for say, the first six months, but if you do not live up to their expectations the strongest early supporters can become difficult and persistent critics.

When you start a new role or project it is always worth being clear what constitutes success in the eyes of your boss or those who have a governance responsibility. Understanding what success means for them at an early stage enables you to brief them on topics of particular interest over succeeding months. It is always helpful to build joint ownership of outcomes with others so there is an alignment of effort, with both you and them viewing success in a similar way. If you and your boss are fully aligned on what success means, you will both be committed to each other's success. The more explicit the shared intent, the better.

It is worth making an assessment about how competitive someone is who you are working with closely. You will want to steer that competitive streak in a constructive direction. If someone is naturally very competitive they may end up not being as committed to your success as you would ideally like. When an over-competitive colleague takes the credit that was properly yours, you may want to revisit what success means for the both of you and how you can be consistently committed to each other's success.[10]

Jo drew a stark contrast between her first two bosses. They both said they were committed to Jo's success, but when it came to the crunch George wanted all the credit for himself, whereas Ken ensured Jo got full credit for her achievements. This experience helped shape Jo's thinking on being clear why people were committed to her success and whether they would be consistent in allowing her to take the credit when things went well.

In practice

- Think through who is committed to your success and why.

- Seek to build a shared focus with colleagues on what success means.

- Recognise the strength of the competitive element in others and how that influences their commitment to your success.

- Be an example by demonstrating commitment to the success of others.

---

10 See *100 Great Building Success Ideas*. Singapore: Marshall Cavendish.

BUILD UP A MENTOR OR THREE

A GOOD MENTORING RELATIONSHIP will enable an honest exchange about ideas and progress.

The idea

A good mentor is someone who has walked a similar path to you and is willing to share their experiences and knowledge. There is a risk of seeking to collect mentors and failing to use conversations with them effectively. In a constructive half hour with a mentor you should not be dumping your problems on them. This would be a self-indulgent way of using precious time with a mentor.

Good preparation is needed to ensure you maximise time spent with a mentor so you are gaining constructively from their experience. A careful choice of topics and questions will enable you to make the most of these meetings. It can be helpful to send a brief e-mail or text in advance saying that you would welcome their perspective on a particular topic.

It is worth asking yourself why someone would want to commit the time to having a mentoring conversation with you. You want the mentoring conversation to be enjoyable and of benefit both to the mentor and you, hence the importance of turning up on time, being positive and explicit in your requests. You might be recounting to them how you had applied what came out of a previous mentoring conversation.

Be ready to respond to a request from a mentor. They may invite you to talk to another colleague or share your views on an issue. Although the mentoring conversation is primarily for your benefit, it is helpful if the mentor feels that they have benefitted too. Perhaps there is some information about what is going on in the organisation that it might be useful to share. Use the time of a mentor carefully so that they are likely to want to see you again, rather than find their diaries too full to fit in another conversation.

Jo had done a couple of pieces of work for the chief operating officer (COO) at the hospital where she was working. She asked tentatively if he would be willing to have a half hour mentoring conversation with her. He said 'yes' without showing huge enthusiasm. Jo started the conversation with a couple of pieces of information that she knew would be of interest to the COO. Jo was then clear about the two topics where she would welcome hearing the perspective of the COO. In her response, Jo emphasised that she understood the relevance of what the COO had been saying. She was explicit in her thanks and ensured the conversation did not overrun. It was a pleasant surprise when the COO said that he would be happy to have a further conversation in a couple of months' time.

In practice

- Whose experience and perspective do you particularly respect who you might approach for a mentoring conversation?

- How will you ensure that such a conversation is used productively?

- How best do you ensure that a mentor gains as much from the conversation as you do as a mentee?

- How willing are you to mentor others in a way that enables you to learn from both being both a mentor and a mentee?

DRAW ON A COACH WHO UNDERSTANDS AND CHALLENGES YOU

In a good coaching conversation you will feel supported and challenged in equal measure.

The idea

In a good coaching conversation you will be growing your strengths and be equipped to tackle demanding challenges effectively. Coaching is not a soft option: it should be both challenging and stretching. The long-term result from coaching ought to be a clear sense of purpose, clarity of aspiration, and focused next steps. The effective delivery of priorities lies at the heart of all great coaching, which follows from productive engagement between the coach, the individual and the sponsor of the coaching.

Good coaching conversations create a space where you can reflect honestly and frankly. The coach is enabling you to explore in depth what is going on, how you are reacting and what your future prospective actions might be. The 'golden thread' running through effective engagement between coach and coachee includes unconditional mutual regard, attentive listening, open-mindedness, adaptability to vary the approach, pace and timing to fit the circumstances, and an emphasis on building creative energy, which enables the coachee to challenge their own thinking and actions in a confidential and secure environment. Good coaching conversations will include a relentless focus on the future, whatever past or current travails there have been.

When choosing a coach you need to ensure that you can build up a quick rapport, respect their experience, and be willing to be open with them. You may want a coach to challenge you directly, or you may want a coaching relationship whereby the coach creates a supportive context and asks questions that enable you to challenge yourself. Always ensure that at the end of a coaching conversation you are clear about the insights gained and how it is influencing your attitudes and actions going forward.[11]

Jo found it easier to work with male bosses than female bosses. She decided to work with a female coach partly to help her think through how she was going to understand and work better with ambitious female bosses. Jo recognised that in some situations she could be defensive when there was every reason to be positive. Jo was clear about the type of areas she wanted to work through with a coach. Jo said to her coach that she wanted to be challenged. They both recognised that Jo needed to be confident in her own strengths and progress before she would be fully willing to challenge herself about her reactions and next steps. The coach was sensitive enough to recognise that she needed to enable Jo to reinforce her confidence, and as a consequence become more adept in dealing with situations where she felt challenged and defensive.

In practice

- See focused coaching as valuable personal development and not an indulgence.

- Be selective in who you decide to work with as your coach so you are both supported and challenged through the conversations.

- Be explicit about how you have reached next steps at the conclusion of a coaching conversation, being clear how you will move on constructively with a confident attitude and clear actions.

---

11 See *Business Coaching: achieving practical results through effective engagement*. Chichester: Capstone (co-authored with Robin Linnecar).

RECOGNISE WHO IS UNLIKELY TO BE AN ALLY

IT IS IMPORTANT TO recognise the reality that not everybody will want to be your friend or your ally.

The idea

You want to be everyone's friend. You are predisposed to be open and seek to bring the best out of others. You might assume that everyone is willing to be your ally. The reality is likely to be that not all your colleagues will want to be your ally. You may be in competition with other teams or organisations that might view you with a degree of suspicion. Your objectives may be in conflict. You may be part of a competitive market where conflict inevitably arises. For example, as a head teacher you want to build a constructive engagement with neighbouring head teachers where there is a shared agenda, but inevitably you are in competition for students—hence there will be a wariness about some forms of cooperation.

If you have been promoted to lead a team, the nature of the ongoing relationship between you and your former peers is a test for both of you. You will want to be open and constructive in the ongoing working relationship, but your former peers may need time to recover from the disappointment of not being promoted. It is possible that they might carry a degree of resentment. For a period they will not be your natural allies: they have to travel on their own journey and it may be ill advised to be over-friendly too quickly. What matters is choosing the right moment when you can begin to work together on a shared agenda.

Sometimes you have to recognise that you will never win someone over. There may be such a difference in approach or personality that means they are never going to become a natural ally. In these cases it is important to have built up enough wider support so that critics of your approach are in the minority. If it reaches a stage where one or two influential people are clearly critical of you and are not your allies, it might be time to move on to another role.

Jo experienced difficulties working effectively with Bob, one of the senior consultants in the hospital. She tried to understand where Bob was coming from. Jo sought to be friendly and constructive but felt rebuffed. Initially Jo felt as though she was the cause of the problem and deliberately tried to modify her ways of working. She recognised that some of the approaches she was advocating were an anathema to Bob. Jo recognised that she had to build allies among the other consultants to try and minimise the effect of Bob's negative comments. Jo learnt to accept she was going to experience Bob as difficult and she had to live with that reality.

In practice

- Do not assume that everyone will want to be your friend.

- If someone is critical of what you are doing, don't immediately assume that you are necessarily wrong.

- Seek to understand why some people won't be your allies.

- Deliberately build allies in situations where people seem to be blocking what you judge to be the right way forward.

BE READY TO FORGIVE AND MOVE ON

WE NEED TO FORGIVE others and ourselves in order to move on and avoid building up resentment in ourselves.

The idea

Someone has let you down. You are cross and frustrated by their behaviour. You resent the way they seem to be unaware of your feelings of being let down. You do not particularly want to forgive the individual and can feel increasingly cross with them. What matters is recognising the nature of your emotional reactions and, ideally, being able to talk through with the individual what went wrong and how you can both move on.

Sometimes forgiveness is about forgiving yourself when you feel you have let others down. There is a risk that we keep beating up ourselves rather than accepting that we have learnt from what has gone wrong and are now moving on. When you feel you have let others down it is important to be able to draw a line under what has happened and know how you will reduce the risk of a similar situation happening again.

If one of your staff lets you down, you want to help them work through what happened in a constructive way so that they are better equipped to handle similar situations in the future. You want to forgive them and 'wipe the slate clean'. The question then becomes how to handle the repetition of similar situations. Forgiveness does not mean forgetting. If someone continually lets you down, or fails to deliver on your expectations, you have an obligation as a leader to take action. If you forgive one 'neighbour' too often it can have a detrimental effect on other 'neighbours': you might be at risk of allowing your forgiveness of one person to appear unfair and inconsiderate to others.

As a leader there are inevitably boundaries to what you can afford to forgive if there are limited signs of a constructive response to what has gone wrong.[12]

Jo became increasingly frustrated with one of the medical consultants who was consistently critical about what the administrators were seeking to do. Jo felt continually misrepresented. Jo tried to forgive this critic because of his strong reputation as a consultant and the difficult personal circumstances he had been through. But Jo felt there were reasonable boundaries to this forgiveness when he kept misusing facts to bolster his points. Jo plucked up the courage to have a couple of frank conversations with the consultant, who did not appear to listen to her. Her sense of forgiveness was being stretched beyond what she thought was reasonable, as this individual's attitude and approach was having a detrimental effect on others.

In practice

- Who do you need to forgive who has let you down to order to help you minimise the resentment you feel?

- How best do you forgive yourself when you have let others down?

- How best do you ensure that you set boundaries to your forgiveness where the forgiveness of one person has a detrimental effect on others?

---

12 See *Effective Christian Leaders in the Global Workplace*. Colorado Springs: Authentic/ Paternoster.

BUILD PEER SUPPORT

PEERS WITH WHOM YOU can have focused 15-minute conversations can be valuable and well worth cultivating.

The idea

I led a programme over a five year period for newly appointed directors of health boards in Scotland. One of the long-term benefits of the programme was the building of strong relationships between peers in different health boards. During the development programme, the directors got to know each other and shared how they were approaching different issues. After the development programme a number of them continued to use each other as sounding boards, which meant they had a different perspective to draw from outside their local context.

When I work with prison governors I encourage them to keep talking with other prison governors about the issues they are facing. As a prison governor it is very difficult to think aloud with your direct reports as anything you say, however tentative, becomes an instruction. It is crucial for a prison governor to have a context where they can develop their thinking without it being immediately interpreted as an order—hence the crucial role of peer support.

A church minister can become trapped by the expectations of their congregation and become blinkered in their approach. What is crucial for a church minister is the opportunity to engage openly and frankly with church leaders in other situations, so they can share experiences and smile about the idiosyncrasies of people in their churches.

Effective peer support does not mean spending three hours together. The focused 15-minute phone conversation can provide an invaluable opportunity to talk an issue through. What is needed is the discipline to set up a conversation, clarity with the agenda and then being committed to following through your conclusions. Good-quality peer conversations may be with people in the same sphere as you, whether you are a health board director, a prison governor or a church minister; or they might be in different spheres and have shared concerns in dealing with the isolation of leadership and living with the expectations of others.

Jo recognised that when she took on responsibility for the operating theatres in a hospital that she needed to build a network with others in similar roles in other hospitals. She was explicit in saying why she wanted to build peer support and believed it would be mutually beneficial. She met up with two people in similar roles and agreed that they would be open to act as sounding boards for each other. These conversations proved valuable in enabling her to stand back and see how other people had tackled similar situations, which gave her new ideas and energy.

In practice

- Be deliberate in building networks with peers in similar roles.

- Take the initiative to prompt conversations with peers and be appreciative about the value of such conversations.

- View setting up a number of sounding boards as a sign of strength and not weakness.

- Accept that as you move into different roles you need to establish different peer networks.

SECTION D
HOW?

CATCH UP WITH YOURSELF

THERE IS A RISK that we have a dated view of who we are and what we can do. Sometimes we need to catch up with ourselves.

The idea

A constant theme in my coaching work is enabling people to 'catch up with themselves'. Often individuals see themselves in the same way as they viewed their capabilities five years ago. Their self-assessment can be frozen in time and, therefore, inaccurate.

It is helpful for any leader to be consistent in applying the values that are important to them and the way they treat and interact with other people. Consistency about values is not about having a fixed view about your strengths and capabilities. Our capabilities are evolving all the time. Each time we chair a meeting, we become better equipped to chair our next meeting. Each time we speak in public we are refining our approach to public speaking.

Catching up with ourselves involves taking the plunge to do things differently and coming out of the shadows in expressing our views more assertively, and then building the experience and our self-belief explicitly into the way we influence others. The more we are willing to move out of our comfort zone, the quicker will be our learning about how we lead in different contexts. We then need to take the second step of internalizing our learning and changing our narrative about the leadership we bring.

When you apply for a job there is often the risk that your description of yourself is about how you entered your current role rather than the leader you would be in the new environment. As a coach, I often find myself helping someone recalibrate what they are now good at, so that their description of their own leadership is up-to-date and pertinent to the situations they are seeking to enter. Catching up with yourself involves being explicit about what attitudes and approaches you are going to leave behind. It is important to seek to forget the anxieties you felt in some previous situations, so that you can enter new situations uninhibited by the past and confident in the approaches you are now able to demonstrate.[13]

James was good at leading projects and had now developed the capability of developing team leaders to run projects well. He was applying for a job where he would have overall accountability for a number of projects. His initial approach was to pitch his case as a successful project manager. His coach prompted him to develop his case based on his effective leadership of project managers, rather than his previous role as a project manager. James spent much of his time encouraging and steering others leading projects: his narrative needed to catch up with what he did now and what would be required of him in this next role.

In practice

- What do others identify as your strengths in your current role?

- To what extent is your description of your strengths out of date and not aligned with how others would describe you?

- With whom can you have conversations to enable you to catch up with yourself and develop a narrative about your leadership that is up-do-date and persuasive?

---

13 See *The Reluctant Leader: coming out of the shadows*. Norwich: Canterbury Press (co-authored with Hilary Douglas).

32 LOOK IN CONTROL

IF YOU LOOK IN control it will encourage others to have confidence in you and what you are seeking to do.

The idea

A leader's behaviour will be mirrored by others. If you look confident, those who work with you are more likely to feel confident. If you look calm, others will react by feeling calm. If you look in control, others will feel more confident about what is happening and less likely to panic about the direction of travel.

You may not always feel in control. There may be lots of uncertainties, which means it is impossible to have any degree of certainty about what is likely to happen next. What you can always control is your attitude to events and your attitude in how you react if things go wrong. If someone feels easily thrown by things going wrong, I encourage them to have an approach whereby they anticipate that, say, three or four things will go wrong each week; they can then prepare their attitude to how they will respond, rather than believing they have to control the situation instantly.

Looking in control is about being ready to steer through different eventualities. It is not necessarily about taking the direct levers of control. It is much more likely to be about equipping and enabling others to handle changing circumstances and unexpected events skilfully.

Looking in control is not about using a deluge of words. Often it involves bringing wise counsel and reflecting carefully about next steps. Looking in control is not about always having the answer, it is about having an approach to finding an answer that others recognise and can embrace.

When James took on his new role leading a team of project managers, he had to get used to the fact that he was not in control of the individual projects. That was not his job. He was in control of how the overall organisation responded to different requests and its developing reputation. He was in control of the timetable and the deployment of the project managers. He was apprehensive about taking on this bigger role and recognised that he was being observed all the time by both his staff and by clients. He needed to look in control so that others accepted his decisions and did not push him unreasonably into directions he did not want to go.

In practice

- Recognise what you can control and what you cannot control.

- Remember you can control your attitude and approach every day.

- Be conscious of the signalling effect of your demeanour and how best you can look in control of what is happening.

- Remember that creating reflective space is entirely consistent with giving signals about being in control of the direction of travel.

REMEMBER YOU ARE ALWAYS PERFORMING A BALANCING ACT

You are forever balancing different considerations when there is no right or wrong answer. Be deliberate in the way you do your balancing act.

The idea

Getting the balance right in the way you work and how you deploy your energy and time is a permanent feature of leading and managing well. There are always choices to be made about when to follow and when to lead. The good leader is always a follower, too, if they are going to use their time and energy well. There is a balance between engagement and detachment. To make a difference you need to be fully engaged, but you need a degree of detachment in order to be objective about what is happening. Sometimes it means going fully into 'engaged' mode, and on other occasions into 'detached' mode.

Some decisions are about principle and others about pragmatism. How best do you hold principle and pragmatism in tension and explain carefully to others how you are balancing those considerations in an appropriate way?

There is a delicate balance between being aware and acting on this awareness. You want to be aware of what is going on without becoming over anxious. You want to be ready to take action when the time is right. There is a balance to be struck between the rational and the emotional, recognising that sometimes we can be too rational for our own good, and on other occasions too swayed by emotional reactions.

There is a balance to be struck between the individual and the collective. Sometimes the onus is on us to deliver. On other occasions, what matters is enabling the team to be fully effective as part of the collective endeavour.

Getting the balance right between being directive and responsive requires an ability to read a situation well and to have a good sense of timing. The success of any leader comes from the capacity to be both directive and responsive in a way that is true to their own values and philosophy, while taking others with them. The good leader brings both realism and optimism. Without realism we are captive to wishful thinking. Without a sense of optimism we are ground down by current reality. [14]

James recognised that subtlety was required of him as a leader. He needed to both give a lead, and follow and endorse the judgements of his team leaders. He needed to be responsive in some situations and directive in others. He needed to be mindful of his reactions to what his team leaders were doing. Getting the balance right was a key part of his role as leader. He had to live with ambiguity in a way he had never been required to do before.

In practice

- Be honest with yourself about the areas where you need to balance your involvement and energy.

- Recognise that the balance between being directive and responsive will keep changing.

- Accept that you will be living with a degree of ambiguity about your changing role; see that as an opportunity for growth rather than a cause of frustration.

- Believe that part of leading well is to follow as well as lead.

---

14 See *Getting the Balance Right: leading and managing well*. Singapore: Marshall Cavendish.

BE CLEAR ABOUT YOUR EXPECTATIONS AND HOW YOU HANDLE THE EXPECTATIONS OF OTHERS

THERE IS AN IMPORTANT balancing act between the expectations you set for others and how you handle expectations others place on you.

The idea

You may well have clear expectations about what people working with you should deliver and how they should be working with others. A risk is that although these expectations are clear in your head, they are not always communicated fully to, or understood by, others. It is always worth spending time working through what are the shared expectations of both you and others.

Being explicit about the expectations that are most important to you, and continually communicating about those expectations so there is no confusion, is important for an organisation's harmony and well-being. Dysfunctional working relationships often result from ambiguity about expectations.

As a leader you can feel oppressed by the apparently never-ending expectations placed on you. There will be expectations from your staff, your peers, your customers and a wide range of stakeholders. It is important to understand where these expectations come from and to be able to protect yourself from unrealistic pressures. It is helpful to think through whether the expectations on you are reasonable in the circumstances, relevant to meeting the overall objectives of the organisation and realistic in their timescale. Regular reassessing of priorities will ensure that expectations do not get out of hand.

The most challenging never-ending expectations are those we put on ourselves, which may come from our own values or psychological needs. The desire to make a difference, or a strong sense of vocation, can mean we build unrealistic expectations and potentially damage our equilibrium. We should always be able to push back when people place unrealistic expectations upon us.[15]

James recognised that he needed to balance setting clear expectations about the quality of work that his managers did while at the same time handling the expectations that were put on him by others in the organisation. He was not just a conduit channelling the expectations of others to his staff, he also had to be a filter in deciding which expectations from elsewhere in the organisation were realistic and reasonable. He needed to ensure that, where he thought the expectations of others were appropriate, that he communicated those expectations clearly in a way that linked them in a co-ordinated way with existing expectations.

In practice

- Think through carefully the expectations you place on others and how you communicate those expectations, recognising that you are going to have to live with never-ending expectations about your contribution.

- Be willing to push back when you think that the expectations of you are unreasonable and unrealistic.

- Seek to link together expectations of key people so there is a coherent narrative both for you and for those you lead.

---

15 See *Living with Never-ending Expectations*. Cambridge: Grove (published late 2017).

BUILD RHYTHMS THAT WORK FOR YOU

BE HONEST WITH YOURSELF in identifying the patterns in the use of time and energy that work best for you.

The idea

Recognising when you are at your most alert to solving difficult problems will help you structure your time to best effect. Your best time to work through difficult problems might be on the commuter train in the morning, or in a conversation with a trusted friend, or maybe while running in the evening. It can be useful to allocate a particular time and place to address difficult problems. Once this time is scheduled, you can tell yourself to stop worrying about a problem, as you have allocated a specific time to address the issue.

Building rhythms that work for you means taking account of your capacity to multitask: perhaps at certain times of day you can handle a number of issues at the same time. It is perfectly legitimate to create space to work through strategic and complicated issues away from other people, with the computer turned off so you are uncluttered by other thoughts.

Leaders who survive best in busy environments are ruthlessly assertive in how they use their time and energy, and in how they vary the pace of each day. They are still accessible to their colleagues, but manage their accessibility and use conversations in a focused way.

A way of building rhythms that work for you could include creating 'shafts of stillness', where you can allow yourself to breathe, relax and cherish good moments. Shafts of stillness can be just five minutes when you turn off your brain. How might you use stillness to calm yourself and move into a different space? Creating shafts of stillness can be an effective way of pacing your energy and keeping events in perspective. What may seem at first like an indulgent luxury can prove to be re-energising and revitalising.[16]

When in his office, James was constantly being interrupted by people seeking his advice. James recognised he needed to be accessible, but he also needed to create time to think through some difficult, longer-term issues. James recognised that he was at his freshest in the morning, in the middle of the week. He experimented with allocating two hours every alternate Tuesday morning for some longer-term thinking. He planned ahead which topics he would address, which enabled him to begin thinking through the problem in advance. James began to observe which activities gave him energy and what sapped his energy, and deliberately began to plan his day to take account of how he used his energy productively.

In practice

- Be explicit about the patterns in the use of time and energy that work best for you.

- Be deliberate in using the time when you are at your most alert to solve difficult problems.

- Be deliberate in setting aside time for longer-term, strategic thinking.

---

16 See *Seizing the Future*. London: Praesta (co-authored with Robin Hindle-Fisher).

BE DELIBERATE IN HOW YOU HANDLE CONFLICT

THE MOST ENERGY SAPPING part of leading well is handling conflict, so it is important to be deliberate in how you handle conflict.

The idea

Conflict, handled well, can be creative. Conflict that leads to emotional angst can be destructive. When conflict is about the open exchange of views and opinions, underpinned by clear analysis, progress can be made, with energy levels raised. Where conflict becomes personal and emotional it saps energy and creates anger and resentment, which destroys a sense of common purpose and does not build new, creative approaches.

The experienced leader will have developed different ways of handling conflict expeditiously. They will have the ability to be able to soak up or ignore criticism, alongside a capacity to debate on equal terms with someone who is in full flow. The thoughtful leader will be able to differentiate between robust, formal, public exchange, and informal or reflective engagement in a private space. When you are in apparent conflict with someone, it is worth reflecting on what type of context you can create where quiet and thoughtful conversation can prosper.

There are times when you have to face conflict head on and be direct in your views, recognising that you will receive verbal criticism. These are the moments to prepare yourself carefully and to enter the conversation with your metaphorical armour-plating on. You may need to be prepared to stick to a predetermined line, even when you are being subjected to painful criticism. A consequence of having been through two or three of these conflictual situations is that you will be better-equipped for next time.

James recognised that one of his customers was disappointed by progress on a major project. James felt badly that he had let the client down while recognising that the client had changed the requirements at a late stage. James accepted that he would have to bear the criticism of the client, but without conceding that it was all the fault of him and his team. He made the point that the client had changed the requirements at a late stage, but did not overplay this argument. James kept his cool in the face of the concern from the client and worked hard to ensure that the working relationship was kept intact for the longer term.

In practice

- See conflict as inevitable for any leader.

- Be prepared for criticism and do not overreact emotionally to it.

- Seek to balance formal and informal exchanges so that a working relationship is not destroyed.

- Recognise that you grow as a leader through the way you handle conflict.

BE ADAPTABLE IN THE WAY YOU LEAD

Doing leadership well requires being adaptable to circumstances and to what is needed from you.

The idea

Leading well involves being both resolute and adaptable. Being resolute is about having the passion to make a difference in uncertain times and a doggedness to keep at it. Passion and purpose start from clarity of intent, consistent underlying values and the importance of building on the imperative for change. Resolution and determination flow from confidence in your values and goals and trust in your own judgement. It involves recognising when you have been given authority by others and being willing to take responsibility for your actions. It combines a strong sense of self-authorising beliefs and actions, with a sound, internal barometer that keeps you on track.

Being adaptable to changing circumstances is a sign of strength and not weakness. Being adaptable includes recognising when persistent action and determination can risk blinkering your understanding of current reality. It includes understanding your emotions and how sometimes you can be too rigid in your reactions. Being adaptable means being focused and retaining boundaries, while bringing a breadth of understanding.

Being adaptable begins from recognising that your experience gives you distinctive insights, and believing you have the responsibility to make choices. To be adaptable involves being open to try new and different approaches and not being restricted by previous frameworks or conceptions. It means not being defined by the expectations of others, and not limiting your perspective about what is successful to earlier definitions.

Living leadership well is about fully embracing your leadership challenges, bringing all your experiences to bear and not trying too hard in a way that makes your approach stilted. When you are living leadership well and balancing being resolute and adaptable, you are better able to judge when to be on the balcony and when to be on the dance-floor—i.e., when to be observing and when to be intervening.[17]

James recognised that he needed to be resolute in ensuring the projects he oversaw were delivered correctly, and adaptable in order to take account of new issues as they arose. New problems were always surfacing and he was having to work continually with his team leaders about the timetable for next steps. James knew that he needed to engage the customers in decisions about timescales so that they felt ownership of the decisions. James had to keep checking that his adaptability was for good reasons and not because he was being pushed around or was afraid of potential conflict.

In practice

- How much do you trust your own judgement in balancing being resolute and being adaptable?

- What opportunities are there for more co-creation, to encourage adaptability while ensuring a strong sense of common purpose?

- When you feel passionate and resolute, how best might you cross-check whether your single-mindedness is well judged?

- Who are your sounding boards to judge whether you are getting the balance right between being adaptable and being resolute?

---

17 See *Living Leadership: finding equilibrium*. London: Praesta.

LEARN FROM OTHER SPHERES

THERE ARE ALWAYS PARALLELS to be drawn from other spheres, such as learning from musicians about giving direction and contributing to the overall impact.

The idea

The conductor of an orchestra, like other leaders, needs to give direction in order to set standards, maintain focus and ensure results. To get the best results they need to engage those they lead, rather than simply requiring them to obey. From this combination, conductors create the conditions whereby the orchestra can bring together their knowledge and skills to make something they could not do on their own. By providing direction along with freedom, and by creating that sense of contributing to the larger whole, conductors and leaders earn the respect, support and loyalty of players and followers.

Chamber musicians play without a conductor. Each player is a voice in the dialogue, sometimes leading, sometimes supporting, sometimes challenging or contrasting, sometimes commenting. The whole is greater than the sum of the parts. All teamwork, be it in a chamber group or in a work context, needs communication and coordination among the team players. Though musicians discuss the music and its interpretation as they prepare their performance, communication in the act of performing is mostly non-verbal. This type of non-verbal communication, the ability to respond almost instinctively to what others are doing, marks high-performing teams.

The audience has a crucial part to play, as musicians sense the listeners' responses and how the music critics are likely to react. For any musician the most serious critics are their fellow musicians. This is equally true for leaders and players in any sphere.[18]

James was sometimes frustrated by the lack of harmony among his team leaders. They did not seem to want to engage with each other in a creative way. He tried to build a strong team dynamic by having away days with them, but this was rarely productive. His response was to pair them up so that they worked together on projects, with an explicit brief to use their respective strengths to good effect. This process of encouraging partnerships began to make headway when a number of his team leaders expressed strong support for this approach. When he got his team leaders together it sometimes felt like a discordant jazz band rather than a harmonious chamber group. James used the music analogy to encourage the team leaders to think about how they wanted to work together going forward, recognising that they needed to embrace both dissonance and harmony.

In practice

- As a leader what is your conducting style?

- How do you combine giving direction with a clear space for people to contribute?

- How might you influence and support team members, including yourself, to get the best out of each other?

---

18 See *Knowing the Score*. London: Praesta (co-authored with Ken Thomson).

RECOGNISE THE POWER OF THE SUMMARY

A GOOD SUMMARY CAN crystallize progress and help unblock next steps.

The idea

Perhaps you can recall a discursive conversation where your energy was dropping. The chair, or an influential contributor, then summarised what had been said and set out simply what might happen next. You were immediately more engaged, your energy levels rose, and you could see a purpose flowing from the conversation.

Developing the capability and confidence to summarise well can radically increase your influence. A good summary will be recognised by others in the room as a valuable intervention. There might also be a sense of relief that someone is willing to grasp what has happened and provide a basis for next steps.

A good summary needs to be accurate, dispassionate and unbiased. When you summarise, you are inevitably being selective in the points you include. When others feel that your summary is helpfully moving a conversation on, they may recognise that it is acceptable that only some of their points are acknowledged. A summary that moves a conversation on is often about encapsulating what has been said so far, thereby giving people time to revisit their thinking about how they build on progress, and move to the next stage.

It is important not to feel hurt if your summary is apparently ignored. It may have fed into people's thinking without their explicitly acknowledging its significance. Do not feel that a summary has to cover every point. A good summary is about catching the essence of the themes and emotions in a conversation.

James often felt trapped between the expectations of senior managers and those of his project leaders. He increasingly recognised the power of the summary in explaining and interpreting the expectations of the leadership team to project managers. He developed the skill of being able to summarize their priorities in a way that the project managers understood and accepted. He also developed a way of crystallizing the concerns and views of his project managers so that he could summarize those perspectives clearly and persuasively to senior management. He recognised that when people began to look bored, he was going into too much detail. He kept coming back to the importance of clarity in deciding on the key points.

In practice

- During a discussion note down two or three key points of agreement and a couple of points for further consideration, and then draw from those points.

- Observe those who summarize well and adopt some of their approaches.

- Think through what is the essence of a point you want to make and how it is likely to be received emotionally.

- Be willing to risk summarizing and do not expect immediate acclaim.

TRUST YOUR INTUITIVE JUDGEMENT

REMEMBER THAT YOUR INTUITIVE judgement is not random. It comes from the accumulation of your experience and expertise.

The idea

Your brain is processing data all the time and linking together new data with earlier experience and insight. What you think about an issue in the moment flows from an immediate, emotional reaction. As your brain and heart reflects on an issue, a more complex process occurs whereby your brain processes new information alongside previous understanding.

Sometimes we need to allow our brain time to process new data. Hence the value of saying that you are going to sleep on an issue and that you will know what you think in the morning. In an active day it can be helpful to withdraw for a few minutes and ask yourself, what do I really think about this? When you ask your mind and heart to focus on a particular question or issue, thoughts and ideas will come to the surface. These thoughts are rarely entirely random— something has set them off.

When you have an intuitive reaction that a particular course of action is needed, you will want to test that reaction through thinking about it further and triangulating your perspective with that of trusted others. Your intuitive sense that there is danger or an opportunity in a particular situation is warning you that there are points that need more attention. Whether there is a sense of emotional excitement or gloom, this emotion provides a clue about what to explore or be wary of.

James had developed an intuitive sense about what was likely to work or not work. He had developed a sequence of questions he used to probe a situation in order to assess whether his intuitive reaction was robust or fanciful. James recognised that he could ask his brain to distil a particular reaction overnight, and by the following morning there was often more clarity in his mind. When the project managers brought ideas to James he would often have initial reactions. He did not want to blurt out those reactions, as it could dampen the enthusiasm and energy of his project managers. James had trained himself to listen to his initial reaction, weigh it up and then talk to others who were knowledgeable in their particular areas.

In practice

- How best do you listen to your intuitive judgements and examine how much substance there is in them?

- How best do you allow your brain to distil your emotional reactions so you both keep an open mind and take those intuitive reactions seriously?

- How can you ensure that your emotional reactions are informing and not distorting your intuitive judgement?

SECTION E
WHEN?

41 SEIZE THE OPPORTUNITY

SEIZING THE FUTURE INVOLVES spotting opportunities and making the most of them.

The idea

Seizing the future demands an upbeat and assertive approach coupled with realism, humility and the confidence to lead by example. It involves standing back, re-evaluating and being liberated from previous frames of reference. The most successful leaders do this while remaining true to their clear, guiding values. Seizing the future successfully requires the key skills of accepting new reality, promoting fresh thinking, ensuring effective engagement, embracing radical approaches and rationing your energies.

Opportunities are always there: you have to focus on finding them. Those who bring insight and perspective and can spot trends and discontinuities will be in a strong position to innovate, and may find their audience more receptive than ever before. Seizing the future requires accepting that conditions have changed and letting go of the past. Embracing new reality needs to start with recognising that the past has gone and adjusting emotionally to what has been 'lost'. Calibrating the gap between the old and the new means being ruthlessly honest about where you are now and the degree of challenge going forward.

Seizing the future means allowing yourself to feel excited by the new landscape. You may feel daunted or dejected, but the new reality can include opportunities. If you adjust the lens, new vistas you never thought possible might open up. You can feel a new sense of liberation and be a source of energy to those around you.

Promoting fresh thinking is about being open, discerning, reflective and liberated, while not devaluing what has gone before. Before you can seize the future you have to accept that life has moved on and that you deliberately take forward your values, experiences and insights into the new landscape.

Freshness of thinking only begins in earnest when you acknowledge what you are feeling about the future. If you are feeling constrained, fresh thinking will not develop. If you are feeling open-minded, fresh ideas can flow in. Key components needed to release fresh thinking include: facing up to the reality of facts and trends; consciously moving your thinking into another place so you are not harking back to a previous era; recognising and removing inhibitors to your thinking; and releasing energy in yourself and others. It involves following your intuition and not always being entirely logical.[19]

Gillian felt the burden of being given additional responsibilities. The government department where she worked was being restructured, with staff numbers reduced. Gillian was sure that there must be opportunities that would flow from this rationalisation and recognised that she had to make some difficult choices. She was convinced that she needed to create enough space in her thinking to identify and take forward opportunities and not be continually on the defensive.

In practice

- What aspects of the past do you need to let go of?

- How do you allow yourself to feel excited about a new landscape?

- What catches your imagination about the future?

- What are the opportunities that might open up going forward?

- How best do you stimulate fresh thinking in yourself and others?

---

19 See *Seizing the Future*. London: Praesta (co-authored with Robin Hindle-Fisher).

42 TREASURE DEFINING MOMENTS

OUR LIVES ARE FULL of defining moments. What matters is how we recognise them and build on them.

The idea

When we understand defining moments it helps us put our work and life into perspective. Often we are going too fast to see the significance of defining moments. Sometimes we are too blinkered to recognise their full impact. It is often only as we look back that we recognise the impact of key moments in our lives. The more we understand ourselves and our reactions and how we are changing, the more integrated and responsive we become as leaders and individuals.

How do we best understand defining moments that are changing our attitudes, beliefs and actions? Living effectively through change is in part about understanding the defining moments in our past experience; but it is also about being willing to embrace the prospect of future defining moments that will enable us to face bigger challenges. To thrive we need to be able to modify our perspective and not be stuck in a rigid and dated world view, while at the same time staying true to our core values.

Defining moments come in all shapes and sizes. Some are dramatic, public events: others are private moments of satisfaction or pain. Moments that give us joy can rush by while painful moments seem to drag on forever. We need to be conscious of living in the moment so we recognise the significance of 'light going on' moments and surprising moments. Sometimes we need to stretch a good moment so we get maximum benefit. On other occasions it is about capturing the moment so we make the most of creative opportunities. An inevitable part of leadership is surviving difficult challenges and then creating future defining moments where we can celebrate progress and ensure that forward momentum is maintained.

Reviewing the defining moments in your life and in your leadership journey offers insights into what has shaped you. As we recognise difficult moments we have survived (be they low points, crisis moments or moments of anger) we equip ourselves for the next steps in our leadership journey. As we treasure good moments we can be confident that we can handle successfully whatever is important to us.[20]

Gillian was apprehensive about how she would lead a team that had been shocked by a difficult rationalisation. The team was grieving for colleagues who had left and were unsure about their own future. Gillian held in her mind how she had handled defining moments before, when she had taken over previous teams at a time of transition. She had coped with difficult reorganisations effectively and moulded new teams who had gone on to greater things. Gillian recognised that she needed to enable future creative moments for her new team, where they could look forward with confidence rather than backwards with pain.

In practice

- What are the defining moments that have shaped you and the way you lead?

- What moments of success do you particularly treasure and how can you hold those moments in your mind as you enter new situations?

- How did you best survive difficult moments and come through them?

- How do you want to forge future moments for your people that are creative and constructive?

---

20 See *Defining Moments: navigating through business and organisational life*. Basingstoke: Palgrave Macmillan.

PACE YOUR INTERVENTIONS

Pacing your interventions enhances the opportunity to have a bigger impact as you carefully choose the moments to intervene.

The idea

The pacing of an intervention can make a big difference to its success. If you intervene too early your words can be lost amidst different introductory contributions. If you leave your intervention too late the direction of travel is already set and your contribution is not likely to influence the outcome. What matters is the quality of your intervention. Interventions that are significant crystallize what is being said and help move the analysis to the next stage. The best of interventions often take the form of a short summary or a key question.

When you intervene you might be aiming to slow down a discussion so there is careful reflection, or you might want to infuse some vision and energy into the conversation when it has lost some momentum.

What matters is being deliberate in the way you intervene in written or oral debate. A stream of consciousness rarely works unless you are deliberately trying to slow a process down and take the heat out of a debate or dialogue. When you decide what type of intervention you want to make it is worth reflecting on the rational and emotional reactions that it is likely to engender. Ideally, each intervention should press both a rational and emotional button as you consider how best to build agreement for a way forward.

Sometimes pacing your interventions involves recognising that there needs to be a sequence of interventions. The first one might be inviting others to think about an issue or recognise a barrier. Subsequent interventions can then develop the thinking where colleagues are already involved in a dialogue. Summarizing progress a little while later will help keep up commitment and momentum. Every intervention is best seen as part of a sequence of interventions, rather than just a one-off contribution.[21]

Gillian was conscious that she had to rebuild the confidence of her team. If she dumped her vision of the future on them they would remain anxious and half-hearted. Gillian recognised that she needed to catch their imagination about what might be possible. Gillian facilitated a cathartic conversation about what needed to be maintained from current practice. She prompted a separate conversation about possibilities for the future and a subsequent one about next steps.

In practice

- Be clear about the outcomes you want to achieve and calibrate the appropriate next steps.

- Plan a sequence of interventions that will take people with you.

- Beware less you dump a set of conclusions on people who need to be persuaded.

- Always be willing to have a sequence of interventions and not rely on one grand intervention.

---

21 See *100 Great Personal Impact Ideas*. Singapore: Marshall Cavendish.

44 TAKE TIME TO REFLECT

REFLECTION IS ESSENTIAL FOR effective leadership. To be reflective is to see the bigger picture, the longer term, and the perspectives that other viewpoints bring.

The idea

To be reflective is to be curious and to ask how others view the issues at hand. Prioritising time for reflection is not a selfish indulgence, it is about ensuring the most demanding issues are addressed and the problems are not ignored. Reflection is about legitimising thinking time. In the contemporary world, leaders need more time to reflect, and not less, because of the rapid pace of change, pressure from the media for instant responses, the risk of emotional over-reaction and the loss of organisational experience and wisdom.

Being a reflective leader requires an acute sense of observation to read what is going on around you. Taking time out to stand and stare can make us feel guilty: we need to resist that reaction. To stand and stare is to observe, to be ready to see the unexpected, to enjoy the ordinary and the predictable, to observe the rhythms of human behaviour and be enthralled or amused by them. Moments to stand and stare give us new energy and help us put the pressures of the day in a wider perspective. Renewed by moments of calm, it can put back a spring in our step.

Being a reflective leader also requires an awareness of what 'lights your fire' and the willingness to see your passions reignited. What 'lights our fire' will change over time. It is helpful to reflect periodically on what inspires us and how we build on a sense of passion for the future.

Sometimes we need our own space to reflect within. On other occasions we need the stimulus of others to bring the best out of us. Essential to thriving as a reflective leader is having good companions who will encourage, support and challenge us. Some of us only realise what we think when we hear ourselves say it. Others do their best thinking quietly, with no one else getting in the way.

Taking time to reflect might involve a two-hour walk away from the office, a dialogue with good colleagues, a thoughtful conversation with a coach, a five minute break between meetings, or a conversation with someone in a very different world dealing with similar issues. We need to work through whether reflection is best done individually or in dialogue with others. What is crucial is that reflective space is created and retained.[22]

Gillian knew that she needed to take some time to reflect on next steps. There were inevitable uncertainties about ministers' expectations for the future. She reflected alone and with her team on possible courses of action. In a reflective, two-hour conversation she prompted her team to talk through what they were passionate about going forward. She gradually built a sense of shared journey, encouraging team members to reflect both individually and as a team about possible future opportunities.

In practice

- Can you allow yourself to stand and stare and review your progress quietly and dispassionately?

- How best can you create reflective space for you and your team?

- How best do you begin to assess what will 'light your fire' going forward?

- If you are an activist, how best can you ensure you value reflective thought and conversation?

---

22 See *The Reflective Leader: standing still to move forward.* Norwich: Canterbury Press (co-authored with Alan Smith).

45 DON'T STAND STILL FOR TOO LONG

It is important to take time to reflect—but standing still for too long risks freezing your attitude and approach.

The idea

On a recent visit to Newfoundland we learnt a lot about maritime history and the sealing industry. We read of sealing parties stranded on ice, with the sealers who survived being those who kept active. Those who stayed still froze to death. Those who survived learned to both conserve their energy and keep moving. Retaining physical movement and emotional hope were essential to their survival.

Moments of standing still are important for us as leaders. We need to observe what is happening around us and be able to stand and stare, though standing on one spot for too long can mean our ideas and attitudes are frozen in time. When we stand still it is about renewing our strength and not about becoming complacent: if we stand still for too long, we may think no other hill is worth climbing. The risk of staying in one place for too long is that possibilities that might once have seemed attainable may now seem to be further away.

When I write a book I will write for 45 minutes and then take a 15-minute break. I need that time to switch my brain off in order to let the creative juices flow; but if I turn my brain off for too long, I lose momentum and cannot keep up the flow of writing. My ideal is a five-hour block of writing time with a 15 minute break every 45 minutes. This balances being completely focused on writing with time to stand still and recharge my ideas. As a leader there are moments when we need to get our team to stand still; but we also need to time this carefully when making decisions about next steps.

Gillian recognised she had to give her team time to adjust to new expectations and lower levels of resources. They needed to adjust emotionally to the new context. Gillian also recognised that the team needed to move on quickly. Gillian calculated that they would need to make decisions within a couple of weeks about how to prioritise next steps. She gave them space to work through the inevitability of decisions, before setting up a summit meeting where decisions were made. She had to push through their reluctance to move forward, believing that it was in the interests of the team that they did not stand still for too long.

In practice

- How best do you apportion your time to balance activity and standing still?

- How long a period of standing still do you need each half day to keep up your energy and resolve?

- How best do you help your team members balance focused activity and standing still?

- What are the danger signals showing people's attitudes and approaches are becoming frozen in time?

USE SHORT CONVERSATIONS THOUGHTFULLY

IN SHORT CONVERSATIONS WE can give clear messages and raise or lower emotional commitment.

The idea

We spend our lives having short conversations with a wide range of people. As with any kind of conversation, it is not just about the words we use, but also our facial expressions and tone of voice matter hugely. Doctors never stop having short conversations. They have learnt to weigh up a situation quickly by watching, listening and asking the right questions.

A good politician knows how to use short conversations effectively in order to demonstrate they are listening and to build up a perspective about the key concerns of their constituents. The good leader is attuned to having short conversations where the objective is to understand the issues people are facing and communicate that they understand and have a clear perspective about where they are leading the organisation.

It is worth thinking deliberately on how you want to use short conversations. There may be a key message you want to leave. Your objective might be to reinforce a good piece of work. Your hope might be to steer someone in a slightly different direction to where they had previously been going.

When you know time is limited, it may be worth saying to a colleague that you only have ten minutes—but they have your sole, undivided attention for that period. When I lead workshops I will often give people short periods of five minutes to coach each other on particular subjects. Workshop members are often surprised how far they can get in five minutes when it is focused around clear questions. Using blocks of five minutes well can have a massive effect on your overall use of time and energy effectively.[23]

Gillian recognised that if she was to motivate her team she needed to engage with them individually. She had a sequence of short conversations with each team member, having set their expectations in advance that each conversation would be 20 minutes. Gillian ensured she was not distracted during each conversation and was conscious of both the content and the emotions expressed. In the last three minutes of each conversation she was deliberately positive about the contribution of the individual going forward. Embedded within each of the short conversations there were one or two practical messages about priorities.

In practice

- Who do you know who uses short conversations well in motivating you?

- How might you use short conversations in a constructive way over the forthcoming week?

- How best might you prepare for short conversations so that your message is focused?

- How best do you ensure that in short conversations you give your sole, undivided attention?

23 See *Conversation Matters: how to engage effectively with one another.* London: Continuum

RESPOND TO EMOTIONAL REACTIONS WITH CARE

Maintaining our equilibrium depends on responding in a measured way to the emotional reactions of others.

The idea

We all tend to have patterns of responses when others have emotional reactions to what we are saying and doing. These reactions are often established in childhood. Harsh words can create an immediate reaction of either anxiety and fear, or an aggressive response. When strong emotions are displayed, we can get into fight or flight mode.

When someone becomes angry with what we have said or done our immediate reaction might be to take things personally. We may think we are in the wrong, even when our actions have been perfectly reasonable and justifiable. An angry reaction might create in us a fear of taking forward the steps we know are essential.

Progress comes through accepting that there will be negative, emotional reactions, and preparing ourselves in how we handle them. It may well be a matter of putting up our defences in advance. It is worth remembering that when someone displays an angry reaction, they are likely to be doing themselves more harm than good. After showing anger, people often regret their words and can then be open to a more conciliatory conversation. It is rarely right to respond to anger with more anger, as this normally inflames a situation. When someone is excessively angry or emotional in their response, it does not mean that the right course of action is to allow that person to have their own way; but it is important to choose the right moment to respond.

When someone has a strong, emotional reaction it is always worth asking why this has occurred and what this indicates about the pressures on the individual. If you are able to treat emotional reactions as valuable data, it helps you understand an emotional reaction rather than being unduly influenced by it. Always keep in mind the question, 'Why is this emotional reaction happening?' It can help you piece together an accurate story about the pressures on an individual and the forces that are driving them.[24]

Gillian was conscious that two of her staff continued to have strong emotional reactions to the reorganisation of the department. Gillian knew that she had to handle them with care, but was also conscious that these two individuals needed to move on in their thinking and their reactions. Gillian prompted an open conversation with them in which they could talk about their emotional reactions and how best they might move on. They welcomed this opportunity for a frank conversation; gradually, they became more attuned to the new context and were better able to handle their emotional reactions.

In practice

- Do not be surprised by strong, emotional reactions at times of change.

- See emotional reactions as providing valuable data about individuals and about the context.

- Recognise how to protect yourself from overreacting to the emotional reactions of others.

- Be willing to create open conversations about moving on from emotional reactions.

---

24 See *Getting the Balance Right: leading and managing well*. Singapore: Marshall Cavendish.

BE WILLING TO TAKE TIME OUT TO DO NOTHING

SOMETIMES THE MOST PRODUCTIVE times are when we do nothing.

The idea

Sometimes the most productive moments are when we are apparently doing nothing, while our physical and emotional energies are being recharged. We may be physically doing nothing but our brain is continuing to process information and emotions.

Often it is right to say to yourself, "I am doing nothing about a particular issue, and I'm not going to overtly think about it for the next few hours." At the same time you are anticipating that the brain will be processing issues and in a few hours' time you might be clearer about the next steps. Deciding to sleep on an issue reflects the reality that the brain is continuing to process information when we are not overtly thinking about it.

We all have different ways of taking time out from thinking about our leadership responsibilities. Doing nothing might be about turning the brain off completely, or it might be doing a physical activity such as mowing the lawn and not focusing on anything in particular. It might involve letting our imagination daydream and seeing where that takes us. Doing nothing might involve practicing the art of meditation and allowing your body and mind to calm down.

What is important is the attitude of mind to doing nothing. The more we can see doing nothing as a way of quietening our hearts and minds so that we can see reality and the future in a more holistic way, the better. Taking time out to do nothing should be a joy and should not be perceived as an indulgence.

Gillian was very committed to the work she did and liked to be active all the time. Gillian could get very tired and recognised that she needed to recharge her batteries more often. Taking time out to do nothing had always seemed like an indulgence, but she now recognised that this was essential to her well-being in the new role. She understood that she needed to give her brain time to work through issues. She wanted to ensure she gave strong, clear leadership, but recognised that she could become frenetic if she was over committed—hence the importance of creating some space each weekend when she did nothing and turned her brain off. During the working week she came to realise that her productivity in the afternoon improved if she switched her brain off from addressing work issues for 20 minutes at some point in the middle of the day.

In practice

- View the periods of doing nothing as important for your well-being.

- Schedule time to turn your brain off during the working day.

- Deliberately park issues and allow the unconscious to take forward your thinking.

- Encourage others to take time out to do nothing and see this as constructive and not an indulgence.

CHOOSE YOUR MOMENT TO RESPOND—AND YOUR ATTITUDE

THERE IS MUCH WE cannot control—but we can control the timing of our responses and our attitude.

The idea

We can sometimes feel that circumstances dictate what is happening to us. We can feel out of control when pressurised by people, politics and circumstances. It is worth reflecting on what you can control, which can be the timing of your response and your attitude. We are making choices every day about how we respond to situations and people. We can let our emotional reactions dominate the way we respond, or we can be deliberate in choosing when and how we respond.

We rarely have to give an instant response. There is normally the opportunity for a five-minute, or even five-hour, reflection. When we feel under pressure it is helpful to create a context where we can stand back, albeit briefly, in order to weigh up the evidence and talk to others whom we trust or whose opinion is important.

Every day we make decisions about our attitude. Henri Nouwen wrote: "Choices make the difference. Two people are in the same accident, but one is severely wounded. They did not choose to be in the accident. It happened to them, but one of them chose to live the experience in bitterness, the other in gratitude. These choices radically influenced their lives and the lives of their family and friends. We have very little control over what happens in our lives, but we have a lot of control how we integrate and remember what happens. It is precisely these spiritual choices that determine whether we live our lives with dignity".[25]

Sometimes we can get locked into a particular attitude towards individuals or a situation. We need to take the time to stand back and be willing to view a situation or person afresh and choose a different attitude. Perhaps we need to bring an attitude that is willing to forgive and move on, rather than being locked into a previous perspective. Having refreshed our attitude, we are then in a much better position to be able to respond constructively going forward.[26]

Gillian viewed her new boss with a degree of apprehension. She tended to respond too quickly to his comments and was not always at her best when in discussion with him. Gillian was clear that she needed to be more deliberate in choosing how and when she responded to her boss. Sometimes she was her own worst enemy when she responded too quickly and could come over as defensive and unsure of herself. Gillian deliberately decided to choose to approach her boss in a more adult-to-adult fashion and not be threatened by his experience or status. Once her attitude became more constructive, she responded to his requests more naturally and in a thoughtful and measured way.

In practice

- Be deliberate about choosing your attitude to people and situations.

- When you think you are going to be tempted by an instant response, take a few moments to stand back before deciding on your attitude and approach.

- If you feel in awe of someone, be mindful whether this distorts how you choose to respond to them.

- Remember that you choose your own attitude to each person, each day.

---

25 See Nouwen, Henri J. *Bread for the Journey*. London: Darton, Longman and Todd, 1996.
26 See *Deciding Well*. Vancouver: Regent College Publishing.

DON'T BE DOMINATED BY THE CONFLICTING EXPECTATIONS OF OTHERS

IF YOU ARE DOMINATED by the expectations of others it can distort your approach, which detrimentally affects your performance and well-being.

The idea

For any leader there will be a range of people who want to exert influence on them. Most of us will be conscious of a conflicting set of expectations that can create confusion and angst. For a team leader there are the expectations of their boss, the operations director, the finance director, their customers, their advisors and their staff. A starting point is to welcome the expectations of others. If there are no expectations, your job is likely to be dull. Managing diversity is critical to making progress.

A key starting point is to be clear whose expectations matter most and how you ensure that you have an accurate perception of those expectations. There is always a risk that what you carry in your mind is a dated view of those expectations, which have moved on in a way that you might not have fully internalised.

Where there are expectations from a customer to whom you do not owe your prime responsibility, it is important to talk through those expectations to enable them to lower their expectations. For example: if you and your team are not going to be able to deliver on a second-order project in the timetable anticipated, the sooner you engage with the customer the better in reassessing what is an appropriate timescale.

Sometimes when people put clear expectations on you it is an opportunity for you to be clear about your expectations of them, to enable you to deliver your part of the bargain. Sometimes expectations are completely fixed because they are part of a formal, agreed contract: but even then there may be scope to work through how they are met and in what order. It is always worth being clear about what is the potential scope for negotiation.

It is helpful to clearly identify the effect that conflicting expectations of others have on you. Is it driving you into behaviours that are distorted, or are you able to hold firmly onto what you think is the right approach to next steps, having taken account of these expectations?

Gillian recognised that there were a range of different views on what her team should deliver over the next phase. Sometimes she woke at 4.00 a.m. worried about how she could meet some of these expectations. Gillian decided that she should be entirely open with her boss about how she addressed these challenges. Together they worked out a plan about how she should prioritise the conflicting expectations, and who she should speak to when expectations were unrealistic.

In practice

- Be deliberate in assessing the realism of conflicting expectations.

- Weigh expectations so you are clear whose views are most important.

- Be open to speaking directly at an early stage to those people whose expectations are not going to be met.

- Ensure that you and your boss are aligned when you give messages to others about expectations that are not going to be delivered.

SECTION F
WHICH?

RECOGNISE WHAT ONLY YOU CAN DO

Recognise what only you can do and focus your contribution in these areas.

The idea

When I coach leaders I often pose the question, 'What is it only you can do to ensure the success of your team?' Being clear about what only you can do will help you prioritise how you spend your time and energy. It is a much more precise question than, 'Where can you add value?' or 'Where would you like to contribute most?'

What only you can do might be about building a key relationship or unlocking an opportunity or making decisions on the allocation of resources. Your team is likely to be able to give you clear feedback about what is the particular contribution they most need from you, which may be about steering the direction of work and giving advice about what is likely to be acceptable to key external interests.

However demanding your role, it will continue to be important for you to do some things you enjoy. It is important to assess different, potential activities in terms of which will give you energy. In other areas of your work, you might want to be role-modelling how things could be done in the future. Such activities do not fall in the category of things only you can do, but role-modelling will have significant benefits for the way individuals in the organisation are going to work at their best going forward.

Bob was delighted to have been appointed as a bishop and was well aware of the weight of expectations on him. He was conscious that he was, in effect, the chief executive of a large organisation, with a mixture of stipendiary and volunteer leadership. He rapidly understood that what only he could do was set the tone for the way the diocese was going to operate going forward. He would need to take the lead on key appointments of senior staff and on the priorities for the diocese. He would be called upon to be the voice of the diocese on a wide range of different issues covering justice and social policy as well as church matters. Bob was clear that he wanted to ensure his senior team members had their own areas of responsibility while recognising that he carried the ultimate responsibility for the reputation of the diocese.

In practice

- Consult others about what they particularly expect from you as a leader.

- Be specific in defining what it is only you can do.

- Recognise that among your range of responsibilities you need to include some things you particularly enjoy doing which will give you energy.

- Reassess on a regular basis whether you need to intervene personally in particular areas to set a direction when activity has stalled and your authority is needed to unblock problems.

52 KEEP REASSESSING YOUR PRIORITIES

Relentlessly reassessing your priorities is essential in order to keep headspace for new priorities.

The idea

Effective leaders prioritise, and then a month later prioritise again. As your staff develop in confidence and competence, more can be expected of them. When one project moves out of a critical phase it may be the moment to pass the lead to someone else. Whenever you can, it is worth keeping an element of wriggle room, so you are operating a little below your full capacity and you can adapt and respond to changing requirements. One approach that works well for some senior leaders is to say they will only be involved in a particular activity for a limited period of weeks during which they are setting the tone and expectations.

If a major project within your area of responsibility is struggling, your choices might be to spend time coaching and steering the key leaders; or, for a phase, you might take on the lead. If you decide to take the lead, it is crucial that you limit the time you give to other areas so that your job remains doable.

When you start a new role you will probably set initial priorities for the first year across all your responsibilities. After a year, you can then take stock and rebalance those priorities. By the end of the first year you will be much clearer about the direction that you want to take the organisation and the liabilities that need to be addressed. A periodic review of priorities is essential if your organisation is going to maintain its momentum and be timely in its contribution and impact. The biggest risk is freezing a set of priorities and not accepting they have become out of date.

Bob was conscious that people across the diocese were committed to a strategic plan, or at least that was what he was told. As he visited churches in the diocese many people he talked to had no idea about what was in the strategic plan. There appeared to be a fixed set of priorities at the centre of the diocese, but little appreciation of these priorities at a grassroots level. Bob recognised that it was timely to review some of the priorities, while recognising a lot of time and energy had been invested in their development. He did not wish to destabilise people who had committed a lot of time and thought to developing priorities, but believed that an updated strategic plan was crucial to maintain momentum within the diocese.

In practice

- Be explicit about your priorities to yourself and others.

- Be open to revising those priorities on a regular basis in the light of new information and relative progress.

- Be willing to give your colleagues more space to take the lead.

- Always communicate clearly how and why your priorities are changing.

53 BE READY TO SWITCH DIRECTION

GOOD LEADERS COMBINE A focus on particular outcomes with a willingness to change direction as circumstances shift.

The idea

The relentless pursuit of a particular goal provides a forward momentum that maximizes the prospect of those goals being delivered. The Olympic athlete is training hard with one goal in mind, which gives them a clear sense of direction. There are moments when we choose to be relentless in the pursuit of goals, and other occasions when it is right to change direction.

The sprinter might decide to focus the second part of their athletic career on distance running. At the conclusion of their athletics career they might move into coaching, administration or the media, or they might decide to move into a completely different arena using their generic skills. An example of someone successful in one career who then used his talents in a different arena is Michael Portillo, who I worked for as a government minister, and who then became a popular TV presenter for programmes on rail journeys, alongside his contribution as a political commentator.

After 32 years working as a senior government official I took a change of direction, moving into coaching, writing and lecturing at the age of 55. My second career was built on the first: I am only able to do what I do now because of my first career. I encourage the people I work with to be open to a change of direction, as it can stimulate new interests and momentum.

A change of direction might relate to the core of your working life, or it might relate to one aspect of your work. It could mean spending a proportion of your time on non-executive director work or contributing in a charitable context, thereby widening your repertoire of experiences and ways of influencing in different contexts.

Sometimes you need to switch direction within your role. As a civil servant I was used to the need to change direction following a national election, when a different political party came into power. Such experiences trained me to be focused on the task in hand, and be open to new directions when there was a major change in leadership.

Bob had enjoyed being a parish priest and then dean of a cathedral in a major English city, leading a diverse staff and making a wider contribution to city life. Becoming a bishop was a change of direction, with responsibilities over a much more dispersed area, where he was setting a tone rather than being responsible for one institution. This change of direction gave Bob new headaches and new opportunities: he was apprehensive at the start, but now welcomed the greater variety in this role.

In practice

- When you are focused relentlessly on one goal, celebrate the momentum that this creates.

- Be open to times when changing direction is right for you.

- Be open to wider possibilities so you can further develop your skills and means of influencing others.

54 KNOW WHAT SUSTAINS YOU

COMMUNICATE, COMMUNICATE AND THEN communicate again.

The idea

You may have spent a long time thinking through an issue or talking about it in a group. A decision is made and you communicate the outcome through an e-mail. You then move on to the next topic, unaware that you have left confusion and uncertainty behind you. When you have dealt with a subject for a while you understand the background and the reasoning that led to a particular decision, but others are hearing the decision without necessarily understanding the context or the reasoning.

Effective communication is not just about knowing the outcome, it is about communicating the rationale that led to that decision. Communication may need to be carefully paced in order to take people with you. Those hearing a message they had not expected may take some time to adjust to the new reality. They may see the problem through very different eyes to yours and not perceive or accept some of your reasoning; hence the importance of clarity in setting out reasons and ensuring those affected by the decision can understand the reasoning, even if they might not fully agree with it.

As a leader you are communicating through your words, actions and demeanour. If you look calm you will be communicating a sense of calmness to those around you. If you are communicating anger or frustration, these emotions will quickly permeate your organisation.

When you have refined your message, repetition is important in the way you communicate. You may become bored with hearing yourself say the same things again and again. But people within and outside your organisation may need to hear the same, consistent messages on a number of occasions before they will internalise the direction of travel and be fully committed to delivering the next steps. Each time you deliver the same message there needs to be consistency in the language and tone, whilst incorporating references to the local context—which means that people accept that you are taking account of their local context.

Bob recognised he needed to make a step-change in the way he communicated the priorities of the diocese. Instead of being required to focus on one big church, there were three hundred churches who looked to him for leadership. Bob needed to send clear, written messages, enthuse senior leaders in the diocese, demonstrate he understood the perspective of individual priests, and be visible across individual churches. He recognised that a key part of his job was to communicate, communicate and communicate again.

In practice

- How best do you use a range of different means to communicate a clear sense of direction?

- What part does social media play within your communication approaches?

- How do you handle becoming bored with communicating the same message?

- What does it mean for you to communicate, communicate and communicate again?

KEEP REINFORCING YOUR LEARNING

WHEN YOU STOP LEARNING it is time to move on.

The idea

After 13 years as an executive coach I am still learning about people and how individuals create opportunities and use them to best effect. Often, at the start of coaching sessions, I ask individuals and team members what they have learnt over the previous couple of months. When they are able to give an energetic response I know that they are engaging well with the opportunities for personal development. I get worried if someone shrugs their shoulders and suggests that they are not learning very much.

If the day job is at a phase where the learning is limited, I invite the team to reflect on what they have learned from their wider activity and how that might equip them for the next steps on their leadership journey. For example, what are they learning about themselves or about enabling change to happen through the contribution they are making in their local community or in their wider family?

One of the delights of working with a number of job share partners is observing how much they learn from each other. In a good job share partnership, the partners are each able to hold in their minds how their job share partner is likely to react in a particular situation. This gives each job share partner two sets of eyes and two types of learning experience.

It is always worth asking yourself the question: how am I embedding my current learning? It might be through continuing to practise different approaches. It could be through seeking focused feedback from others about what is working well or less well. It could involve discussing your learning with a trusted colleague, mentor or a coach. It is my observation that reinforcing learning rarely comes through long courses, but focused activities (half day to five days) can be powerful in helping crystallize learning and shaping your approach. Investing in your learning and setting clear objectives, with a follow-up opportunity to reinforce that learning, is rarely wasted.

Bob recognised that he needed to make a mental shift, as he was now chief executive of a dispersed organisation. He talked to leaders in similar situations in the private and public sector. Bob learnt a lot about creating a sense of direction and communicating effectively by talking to regional leads in both government and banking organisations. Bob was part of a cell group of newly appointed bishops who shared openly their experiences and were able to reinforce each other's learning. Bob found that frank and challenging conversations with a coach helped him clarify his own next steps on difficult issues.

In practice

- What have your learnt about yourself over the last three months?

- What are you seeking to learn over the next three months and how will you assess that learning?

- How best do you crystallize your learning: is it through writing it down or talking it through with others?

- How best do you use a coach or mentor to help define your learning?

- What type of short course might help take your learning into its next phase?

56 KEEP COACHING AND INVESTING IN OTHERS

Your legacy is the people who succeed you.

The idea

The good manager or leader is focused on bringing the best out of their people. A crucial skill is being able to use coaching effectively to draw out the capabilities of those working for you. In a fast-moving world, coaching skills are an essential prerequisite of good leadership and management. They are not an optional extra. The good leader who brings the best out in their people will use a range of coaching approaches and will focus their use when staff are facing transition or needing to step up to new challenges.

Using coaching approaches well depends on you being willing to stand back and not always be in direct control. Success comes through enabling others to renew and reframe, and to be refocused and re-energised. Using a coaching approach can be a liberating experience. It will release you from feeling you have to solve every problem yourself. Applying a coaching approach is just as demanding as leading a project yourself, but in a very different way. The ability to ask the right questions and bring different insights becomes much more important than finding a solution.

The leader who coaches well is able to conserve their mental, emotional and physical energy so it can be deployed when it is most effective. Bringing out the best in others will enable you to bring out the best in yourself, as you can then focus more readily on what you can do to ensure the success of a particular endeavour.

Viewing your coaching of people in your organisation as an investment helps reinforce the value of spending time and energy in this way, while recognising that it can take time for this investment to lead to outcomes. If someone is going to learn and grow effectively they will need plenty of practice and may well learn more through their failures than their successes. Investing in others might mean a short-term hit in order to ensure a long-term gain. Time invested in coaching is rarely wasted, but it does need to be used purposefully and selectively. It helps if there is clarity about the outcomes at the end of a good-quality coaching conversation, with specific next steps.[27]

Bob was conscious that he needed to devote time to develop his senior staff. A couple of them had the potential to move into more senior roles. He committed time to help stretch their thinking and ensure that they were able to view issues from a wider perspective. Two other members of his team looked a bit downcast. Bob wanted to revitalise them: hence he deliberately spent time talking with them about what might catch their imagination and how he and they could invest effectively in their future.

In practice

- How best can you develop and invest in your own coaching approach?

- Where do you need to invest in others to fulfil their long-term potential?

- Who do you need to spend time coaching to help revitalise them in their next steps?

- How can you use focused coaching, time and conversations to best effect?

---

27 See *100 Great Coaching Ideas*. Singapore: Marshall Cavendish.

57 BUILD YOUR SUCCESSION

Every leader has a duty to develop people who can succeed them.

The idea

The insecure leader may well want to give the impression they are irreplaceable. They fear that developing others who can be their successors could mean they have to exit their current role sooner than they would choose. To have a successor in waiting can mean you act defensively because you are threatened by their presence.

The mature leader will delight in the presence of good people working for them who can progress into a senior role. When you have developed one or more people who could succeed you, this gives you a superb opportunity to develop your contribution elsewhere in the organisation or more widely. It should be a liberator, and not an inhibitor, of your own contribution and development.

Developing your own succession might involve identifying those with potential within the organisation in whom you want to invest. This might involve seconding them elsewhere to widen their experience, so that their candidacy is strengthened through this wider experience. Developing someone's credentials as a leader can mean them substituting for you at key meetings or when you are away. You may want to give them sole charge of a particular area so they can practice the art of leading at a more senior level.

Ensuring effective succession might also mean looking outside your organisation to identify individuals who can make a significant contribution as a team member and then bring a mix of expertise that can equip them to succeed you. Building your succession is not just about one person. Ideally, it means developing two or three people as potential candidates. Circumstances may dictate that one or other is more suitable when it comes to filling the vacancy. Your rationale for the two or three individuals is that you are helping develop them for a range of more senior roles, and not just as a potential successor to you.

When Bob was dean of a cathedral he invested in two of the residentiary canons as potential successors, and mentored a couple of other church leaders who were regarded as potential cathedral deans. He viewed the time committed to these four people as important, both for the individuals and for the wider Church. When Bob became a bishop, all four applied for his dean position, and one of the external applicants was appointed. Bob took a lot of satisfaction from having contributed to generating a strong field for the post.

In practice

- Be thoughtful if you are hesitant about having a potential successor working for you.

- See spending time with potential successors, both inside and outside the organisation, as a key investment.

- Treat potential successors equally and be wary if you have favourites.

- Develop potential successors for a range of senior posts, and not just yours.

BE WILLING TO TAKE HARD DECISIONS

WHEN YOU HAVE MADE two or three hard decisions subsequent ones become more straightforward.

The idea

Whenever you take on a new role there are inevitably hard decisions to make. Perhaps your predecessor had put off some decisions on the basis that the new incumbent could make them. Perhaps your predecessor felt that these decisions had been too difficult to take because of the investment by people in the organisation.

When you start a new role, you will view it more objectively than in 12 months' time. After three to six months you know enough about the context to be able to make informed decisions about people's situations: a few months later your emotional reactions will have become less objective and more influenced by your own investment of time and energy.

When I coach individuals, I ask them at the six month point: what hard decisions do they now need to take? This may be about strategic direction, priorities or people. There may have been an accretion of priorities under previous leadership that now need to be rationalised. The previous leader might have been personally committed to some individuals whose performance the current leader judges is less important over the next phase.

Getting people to accept hard decisions may require you to be direct and have painful conversations. You may, as a consequence, face criticism and a strong emotional reaction. You may be accused of destroying what has been built up. You may need to be prepared for a harsh and critical reaction.

When you judge that hard decisions are needed it is helpful if you can talk them through with trusted others. This might be your boss or the chair, or it could be a trusted colleague or a coach. It is important to seek to anticipate the likely reactions to hard decisions so you can be prepared in your responses. When hard decisions need to be made in relation to people it is important to find, if possible, a constructive way forward for the individuals so they can move on with honour and enter their next space positively.

Bob soon recognised that one of his senior staff was struggling and not having the impact required. Bob was clear he needed to encourage this person to move on. He started with a gentle conversation about future possibilities in which the individual showed no inclination to move on. After further critical comments from others about the contribution of this individual, Bob decided that a more direct conversation was needed. Bob collected evidence of concerns and shared them in a calm and thoughtful way with the colleague who was struggling, who left the meeting thoughtful and open to creating a different future for himself. A few months later, this individual's departure was announced, even though his next role had not been finalised.

In practice

- What two or three hard decisions do you now need to make?

- What is holding you back from making these decisions?

- How can you best prepare yourself for hard conversations with teams or individuals?

- Who can you talk through these decisions with in a way that will strengthen your resolve?

59 INVEST IN BUILDING TEAMS

WHEN A TEAM IS working well, productivity is high, individual differences are recognised and successes are celebrated and shared.

The idea

Ensuring that a team is effective requires balancing action and reflection. Teams benefit greatly from learning from each other's experience, and translating that into new ways of working. Observing when teams make a difference to overall outcomes enables you to develop your understanding of why teams matter. Reflecting on when a team can help you be effective can sharpen your understanding about what makes a good team and your commitment to make a team work well.

A team may appear to be working effectively; but exploring where a team is not maximising its potential can provide revealing insights for any new team leader or member. Understanding which teams have adapted well to changing circumstances gives a clear insight into the characteristics of teams that are likely to continue to be effective. Recalling when you helped turn a team around reinforces your recognition of your capability to influence others.

It is worth consolidating what you learnt from teams that have not fulfilled their potential. Perhaps their effectiveness has been eroded by communication problems, or it has been overwhelmed by information or defeated by rapidly evolving circumstances.

Keeping investing in teams you lead might involve regular stocktakes at the end of meetings, articulating what you observe, encouraging input from different specialists, ensuring the voice of the customer is never far away, and encouraging interchangeability of roles where possible. It is worth being deliberate about how you invest in your team. You will want to ensure, if possible, the right type of mix of people. As new people are appointed, you ideally want them to complement the skills and approach of people already in the team.

It is helpful to set aside time for team members to reflect on their respective strengths. When I work with teams, I invite team members to say what they would most appreciate from their colleagues in order to bring the best out of them. I invite them to be open about the type of contribution they would like to bring to the team going forward. You may want team members to work together bilaterally on issues of shared interest. The stronger the linkages between team members, the stronger and more coherent the team is likely to be.[28]

Bob observed that his senior team members were more concerned about leading their individual functions than contributing across wider priorities. Bob initiated a review of the strategic priorities and invited his senior team to take responsibility for different cross-cutting aspects. Bob arranged a half day where some psychometric results were shared. Bob prompted a conversation about how the senior team could bring the best out of each other going forward. It was hard work, as two of the senior team members were very reluctant to participate.

In practice

- Prompt conversation about what can be best achieved as a team rather than individually.

- Celebrate the varying types of contribution from different team members.

- Create enough space for team members to reflect together on what has worked well or less well.

- Create informal moments for team members to get to know each other better.

---

28 See *100 Great Team Effectiveness Ideas*. Singapore: Marshall Cavendish.

RECOGNISE THAT YOU LEARN MORE FROM FAILURES THAN SUCCESSES

WE ARE SHAPED BY our failures. We are reinforced by our successes.

The idea

Our failures can sink us or strengthen us. An acute failure may mean the end of our job, but we will have learnt hugely from the experience and be better equipped for whatever the future holds for us. Life is full of small failures; the target which we did not quite reach, the timetable which was not entirely accurate, the paper that was criticised for missing out a couple of points.

We need to accept that failure is part of life. We can learn a great deal from major failures about our priorities and approach. Living with small failures is about continuous learning and accepting that if it is 80 percent right, then that is good enough in many situations. We can have a distorted view about the levels of attainment that are necessary. We might want to achieve 'A' grade for everything when a 'B' grade performance across a range of areas is more than adequate. Striving for perfection can lead to distortion in our use of time and energy.

The degree of tolerance for failure will vary from one subject to another. Crossing the road without being knocked over requires a 100 percent successful completion. But if you are getting agreement for 80 percent of your proposals, that may be a very high success rate when tendering for contracts.

When you are responsible for actions that are deemed to have failed, how you respond and learn is crucial. If you see failure as a time of significant learning you can turn failure to constructive outcomes. If you become overwhelmed by your own failures there is a risk of going into a spiral of hesitancy and disenchantment.

The scientist sees every failed experiment as a success. They have learned that a specific approach is not providing a constructive answer. This is why our failures are as important as our successes.

Bob was conscious that one of his early appointments had not worked as well as he had hoped. The question was, did he persevere with this appointment or transfer responsibilities elsewhere? He decided to talk in an open way with the individual concerned, who also felt that the new responsibilities had not worked well. They decided together that it was right to make a further change in responsibilities rather than persevere with the current arrangements. They both recognised that what was now seen as a minor failure could easily become a much bigger problem, which was in neither of their interests. Bob was pleased that he had sought to tackle this issue at an early stage and not let it fester and become acute.

In practice

- What are the failures you have learnt from most?

- How best do you share your own experiences so that others see learning from failures is an inevitable part of the leadership journey?

- How best do you equip your team to learn from their failures as much as their successes?

- What potential failures within your area of responsibility do you need to address now, before they become acute?

SECTION G
WHERE?

TAKE PRIDE IN THE SUCCESS OF OTHERS

TAKING PRIDE IN THE success of others gives you huge, personal satisfaction and reinforces the value of the mentoring you are able to give.

The idea

I recently spoke with Jim Houston, who was Principal of Regent College, Vancouver, when I was there as a postgraduate student in 1970. Jim is now 93 years of age and takes huge pride in hearing stories about the lives of his former students. Jim inspired me to explore the possibility of a career in government. He also sowed seeds in my mind in 1971 about writing books. It took time for this seed to germinate, as my first book was published 33 years later, in 2004.

Each of us will have had mentors who believed in us and took pride in our progress. These mentors may have been family members, teachers, or members of the local community as we grew up. We can honour their commitment to us in different ways, perhaps through taking time to write to or meet up with those who have mentored us over the years. It is right to allow those who have been key influences on our lives to take pride in our life journeys.

As we invest time and energy in others, we may not see results for a long period: as we engage with someone through difficult times we may see little apparent progress. But those with whom we have stood alongside through tough times may treasure the shared experiences. When you reconnect with those you have led or mentored, allow yourself to take pride in their success. Your strongest legacy may well be the next generation of leaders who you have helped to nurture and grow.[29]

Mustaq was a middle manager in an engineering company who did not feel his career had progressed as well as he had hoped: sometimes he felt an element of disappointment. But Mustaq did take pride in the way his apprentices had matured. These apprentices started their training with limited self-discipline and self-awareness. Mustaq's approach caught their imagination and they quickly became more disciplined and keen to learn. Some had moved into management and a couple had been promoted ahead of Mustaq. He was delighted by their success. Whenever he felt disappointed by his own progression he remembered his joy in seeing how his apprentices and mentees had matured as technicians and successfully moved into management roles.

In practice

- Who has taken pride in your success and how can you acknowledge their contribution?

- Who have you influenced in a way that has contributed to their development and confidence?

- How do you respond to someone you want to encourage who is unresponsive?

---

29 See *The Emerging Leader: stepping up in leadership*. Norwich: Canterbury Press (co-authored with Colin Shaw).

62   BE READY TO MOVE ON

HOWEVER COMMITTED AND SETTLED you are in your current role it is helpful to think through how ready you are to move on.

The idea

In my coaching work I encourage people to have an open mind to the possibility of moving on. However engaged you are in your current work there is no guarantee that it will continue in its existing form. Economic and political circumstances may mean that your current role comes to an end. However much you enjoy being an officer on a merchant ship, or a manager at a coalmine, or a manager in a government organisation, the time may come, maybe sooner than you had hoped, when your job no longer exists.

Your fear might be that if you see your job as temporary you would be less committed to it and gain less fulfilment from it. The more you view each role as a time of continuous learning and an opportunity to influence the development of others, the less likely you are to be blinkered that this is the only job for you. We can become so fixated on a particular career or vocation that we see moving on as a failure and not a new beginning.

Those who have been most successful in commerce, government service, or charities have often been those willing to learn and then move on. The bosses I learnt most from brought experience from different worlds into the next phase of their leadership journeys.

Being ready to move on means being fully committed to your current leadership role while bearing it lightly. It involves being utterly realistic in assessing the economic and political context in which your organisation is operating, and scanning the horizon and being prepared to 'jump ship' if necessary. Being ready to move on is not defeatist, it is accepting reality.

Mustaq recognised that part of his disappointment flowed from how his protégés had progressed to more senior levels. Mustaq was dejected about his prospects, although he was continually told he was making a valuable contribution. He was able to take pride in the engineering projects he was leading, but he was not convinced that he would ever be promoted within this organisation. He was fully committed to all the projects he was engaged with, but recognised that he had to be willing to 'cut the ties' and move on if he was to progress. Reality hit home hard when another of his former protégés was promoted above him. For Mustaq this clarified the imperative for him to be ready to move.

In practice

- What do you observe about the career journeys of those who have been willing to move from organisation to organisation? When has it worked well or less well?

- What do you observe about what has happened to those people who have moved on from similar roles to you?

- What will help you become more open-minded about moving on from your current role?

- What could happen over the next few months that might force you to make a decision about moving on?

BE OPEN TO A NEW BEGINNING

WE CAN AND SHOULD be open to new beginnings at any point in life. This keeps us fresh and alert to possibilities.

The idea

Whenever someone is feeling low about how their experience and skills might be relevant in other spheres, I encourage them to identify the generic skills they will bring to the next phase of their life journey. I invite them to think through what other strengths and skills they have. How capable are they in influencing others, and how effective are they in bringing projects to a conclusion? Often, there is a litany of skills and qualities that an individual takes for granted and does not see as transferable. They undervalue their ability to crystallize arguments, influence others effectively, and move projects to completion, which is a hugely valuable skillset that can be applied to good effect in a range of different contexts.

Being ready for a new beginning means combining an accurate assessment of your expertise alongside a realism about what is possible. I had loved the mentoring work I had done as a director general and saw an opportunity to build on those mentoring and coaching skills when I moved on from my first career in government. I joined a coaching organisation, initially on secondment, and relished this new beginning in my mid-50s. I encourage the people I coach to see new beginnings as potentially opening up a new phase of life—which could be into a new career, or moving on to a similar role in a different part of the organisation, or a different organisation. I encourage them to be curious about possibilities and open to exploring new opportunities. The new beginning in executive coaching lifted my energy. We all need new beginnings periodically to bring the best out of us and keep us stimulated for the next phase of our life journey.[30]

Mustaq recognised that he needed to think seriously about moving on. A couple of colleagues had moved to other organisations and encouraged him to follow them. He tentatively got in contact with them and was soon being sought after. He decided to move to another organisation in the same vicinity. Changing jobs was less painful than he expected, as he found he enjoyed working with his new colleagues and felt that his expertise was valued. He observed a new confidence in himself and reflected on the constructive and far-sighted contributions he was making. His previous sense of disappointment was being replaced by a sense of excitement and anticipation.

In practice

- What type of new beginning are you open to, and how radical might that be?

- What are the generic skills that you can take forward into your next role?

- What future possibilities might excite you?

- Who do you know who will help you talk through ideas for the future?

---

30 See *Finding Your Future: the second time around*. London: Darton, Longman and Todd.

RECOGNISE WHEN YOU ARE GETTING BORED

OUR ENERGY LEVELS ARE a good indicator of the fulfilment and stimulus we are getting out of a particular role.

The idea

There can be a range of different reasons why you are becoming bored in a particular role. It might be because the work is repetitive and simply boring. As a lawyer you might be being given similar cases all the time. The boredom might flow from a lack of appreciation from your boss and other colleagues and from a frustration that there is limited progress. The boredom might be a consequence of your own physical tiredness, which means that your level of curiosity and engagement is low. Your boredom might be a consequence of being in a job for too long and having been through a similar cycle of tasks on a number of occasions.

Sometimes we do not recognise that we are getting bored. What we do observe is that our energy levels gradually decline and our commitment to ensure progress is easily diminished. Sometimes we have to ask ourselves whether we are getting bored with the work and what are the reasons for that boredom.

Some of the reasons for boredom can be easily tackled. Adding in some more interesting tasks to a job that includes a lot of routine activity can kick-start energy levels. Being explicit about the type of appreciation you need can put your energy levels up a few notches. Investing more time in helping the personal development of your staff by allocating responsibilities, rather than doing the work yourself, can give you a new level of satisfaction.

There are times when it is helpful to be going through a more routine phase at work, such as when your personal and family life is busy. On these occasions, recognising that a less demanding role is exactly what is needed enables you to have the energy to fulfil other responsibilities. What is important is that you do not fall into an acceptance that doing just an adequate job is going to be fully satisfying over the longer term.

Mustaq recognised that his new job had repetitive elements to it. There was quite a lot of routine work that had to be done well: Mustaq recognised that a key part of his assessment would be whether he was able to do the repetitive work effectively. Mustaq saw other aspects of his new role as exciting, giving him an opportunity to contribute on a wider platform than he had been used to. Mustaq was clear that he needed to hold together each aspect of his role and make a success of both the relatively boring and the more creative parts of his job.

In practice

- What do you observe about how people handle repetitive jobs effectively?

- When your job feels boring, how do you ensure you keep up your commitment and energy?

- How can you ensure that there are elements of your work where you are able to exercise your curiosity and your ability to bring the best out of others?

65 RECOGNISE WHERE YOUR RESPONSIBILITY LIES

Recognising your responsibilities is a duty not to be ignored—but an overdeveloped sense of responsibility can be destructive to your well-being and effectiveness.

The idea

We pride ourselves on the freedom we have, but can be hesitant about taking full responsibility for our actions. We like the freedom to choose how we spend our time and energy, but we can too readily place the responsibility on others when things go wrong.

Exercising choice means accepting responsibility for our actions. When we have been appointed to a role, it is perfectly reasonable that we are held accountable for the exercise of our responsibilities and the delivery of agreed outcomes.

Having overall accountability does not mean we have responsibility for every individual action. When we lead a team well we are motivating others and bringing clarity about respective responsibilities. We are providing overall direction and making clear what our direct reports are responsible for delivering. Our responsibility is then to create a constructive culture, provide early warning about wider issues, and ensure cover when the work of the team is criticised by other parties. It is not your role to do the jobs of your staff or to take back the responsibility that you have delegated to them. Taking back responsibilities prematurely clogs up your diary and absorbs your intellectual and emotional resources to an unreasonable extent. There are inevitably moments of emergency when you have to intervene, but this should be the exception rather than the rule.

Mustaq was exceptionally good as a technical engineer. There was always a risk that his staff would delegate things upwards to him. Mustaq wanted to help his staff, but was mindful that the responsibility for individual projects should stay with the project leaders. His role was to mentor and guide and not to do the technical work delegated to others. Mustaq had to be disciplined with himself to ensure he did not do the work that was properly the responsibility of his staff.

In practice

- Recognise what are your overall accountabilities and be clear to whom you have given responsibility for delivering particular outcomes.

- Articulate clearly where you judge your responsibilities and the respective responsibilities of your staff lie.

- Be mindful if others try to upward delegate their responsibilities to you.

- Be willing to take over others' responsibilities in an emergency, but ensure that responsibilities return to the appropriate people in due time.

- Be ready to stand back and reassess if you feel overburdened by particular responsibilities.

ACCEPT THAT THOSE CLOSEST TO YOU HAVE PREFERRED DESTINATIONS

However strong your sense of vocation, it is important to give equal weight to the preferred destinations of those closest to you.

The idea

When I was in my twenties and thirties, most householders had a prime breadwinner, with one spouse (normally the wife) content to do lower paid and often part-time work, or be fully committed to charitable or church leadership activities. In the current era it is much more likely that both partners are doing busy and demanding work.

When the arrangements for a couple in busy roles are working well, there is an awareness of the respective pressures and an understanding about respective aspirations and preferred destinations. I have seen successful partnerships where two individuals have taken it in turn to focus on demanding leadership roles. These arrangements only work when there is a deep, mutual respect about the career choices and preferred destinations of both people.

Parents who are successful in their careers will inevitably have aspirations for their children. Teenagers can feel under huge pressure of expectation when their parents have been successful. They have grown used to the trappings of financial well-being, but are not sure whether they want to live with a similar pressure to that experienced by their parents. So their preferred destinations may be very different to those of their parents.

You want your staff to be equally as good as you. Well, not quite as good, perhaps—or one of them might be appointed to replace you earlier than you would like. The wise leader does not expect their staff to mimic them. The wise leader wants each member of staff to develop their skills and bring the leadership approach that works effectively for them. The astute leader's aim is not to create followers in their own image. Their intent is to help create the next generation of leaders, who will bring their own understanding, perspective and energy to take the leadership into its next phase.

Mustaq recognised that the team he led included some who aspired to be technical experts and others who wanted to move into management roles. Mustaq was astute enough to avoid advocating one particular model of success. He encouraged his staff to think in an open-minded way about their future and to develop their own thinking about preferred destinations and not be channelled along one particular route.

When Mustaq moved into a new role he had open conversations with Naheed, his wife, in which they talked about their respective aspirations and how they complemented each other. Naheed thoroughly enjoyed her garden design work, which built on her creative strengths. Mustaq and Naheed could fully see their careers as complementary for the next phase of their lives, while recognising they were both likely to go through busy periods.

In practice

- How open are you with those closest to you about your respective, preferred destinations?

- Might you be perceived as imposing your preferred destination on those closest to you?

- How best do you let those closest to you develop clarity about their preferred destinations without feeling unreasonable pressure?

KNOW WHAT STIMULATES YOUR IMAGINATION AND CURIOSITY

We cannot simply switch on our imagination and curiosity, but we can put ourselves into contexts that enable us to be imaginative.

The idea

When are you at your most creative? Perhaps that depends on your mood, your energy levels, your relative freedom from distractions, as well as the prompting you receive from what you hear and see. My imagination is at its most creative when I am on a long-distance walk, taking in open views and a strong sense of journey. I delight in the wind blowing on my face and the sense of progression as I move through one field and into another. I see shapes in the landscape and hear sounds that prompt me to think afresh about issues I have been wrestling with. A long walk in the countryside allows me to engage with all five senses of seeing the landscape, hearing the birds, feeling the wind, smelling the fresh grass and tasting the rain as it drips off my rain hat.[31]

For others, engaging with their senses in different ways stimulates their imagination, be it through listening to a Mozart violin concerto, watching a Shakespeare play, tasting fresh Beaujolais, smelling fresh azalea plants or touching fine fabric.

As we read books or articles in which others share their journey, we can sense new horizons opening up that can stretch our thinking about what is possible. When coaching, I will sometimes say, 'Imagine what might happen if you were able to overcome the next obstacle you are facing.' When someone has developed a clear sense of what they want to be doing or expressing after the next obstacle has been overcome, they can find new courage to progress beyond the next obstacle. Once their imagination has latched onto a possible future state, this pulls them through a difficult period.

Mustaq tried to persuade some of the young technicians that they could become qualified engineers and was surprised by their lack of ambition. When he talked with them individually, he encouraged them to think about the type of job satisfaction they would have once they were fully qualified. Mustaq encouraged them to anticipate the freedom and greater engagement they would then enjoy, and encouraged them to be curious about what might be possible. When a couple of them began to see potential opportunities, they became more engaged with the study necessary to attain the qualifications required for advancement.

In practice

- How best do you use your five senses in stretching your imagination about what is possible going forward?

- When is your imagination at its most constructive and how can you cultivate more occasions when your imagination is stretched?

- How might you encourage others to use their imagination constructively?

---

31 See *Celebrating your Senses*. Delhi: ISPCK.

ALLOW YOURSELF TO TAKE PLEASURE IN RECOGNITION

APPRECIATE RECOGNITION AND DO not be dismissive of it.

The idea

When you are recognised and praised by others, your first reaction might be one of embarrassment. You want to move on quickly because you feel uncomfortable. But it is not indulgent to enjoy your moment in the limelight. When your contribution is recognised publicly, it will give huge pleasure to those who contributed to that outcome. You do not want to deprive these individuals of the reflected glory that they can share in. On the other hand, it is not helpful to crave for recognition or to be self-indulgent in seeing recognition as the culmination of all you have striven for.

I am writing this book at the time of the 2016 Rio Olympics, with a number of athletes winning medals for the second or third Olympics in succession. They enjoyed the recognition in 2008 and 2012, and then buckled down to the rigor of training, which has enabled them to be successful again. These Olympians provide a powerful example of a disciplined focus to reach a goal, despite previous achievements.

The good leader ensures that the contribution of each member of their team is recognised and celebrated. Recognition is not about offering platitudes and benign generalities. The best sort of recognition is specific in acknowledging the nature of the individual and team contribution. Allow people to enjoy recognition without imposing immediately the next demanding task on them. Allow and reinforce those moments of pleasure and satisfaction before creating the next set of expectations.

Mustaq was modest and self-effacing and did not like the limelight. He tended to bow his head when his work was being praised. When the work of his team led to an award, he recognised that he needed to be upfront and confident when his team received the award. Mustaq recognised that he needed to demonstrate that he was taking great pride in the contribution that his team had made. Once he had let go of his reservations, he had a broad smile and enjoyed the recognition that he and his team now received.

In practice

- What holds you back from enjoying recognition?

- How can you ensure that you allow others to share in the recognition given to you?

- How best do you recognise the contribution of your team in a way that rings true for you?

- How best do you ensure that recognition leads to the next adventure and not to complacency?

CREATE EXPECTATIONS BUT DO NOT BE RULED BY THEM

SETTING CLEAR OBJECTIVES PROVIDES focus for both you and others, but it is important to be aware of the risk of being overwhelmed by expectations.

The idea

It can be helpful to create expectations for yourself and others about what is possible. A clear target or milestone helps focus the mind in using time and energy well to deliver on key outcomes. Shared expectations in a team help prompt a sense of common purpose and shared endeavour.

However, putting too many expectations on yourself can create a burden that pushes you down rather than stretches you forward. There is a delicate balance between setting expectations that will motivate and align you and colleagues, while avoiding expectation fatigue. One answer is to limit the number of expectations to key priorities—or else only a proportion of expectations will be met. Revising expectations in the light of progress is always necessary and is an expression of realism and not weakness.

It is worth reflecting on the source of the expectations. Have they come from other people, or are you imposing a tighter set of expectations than is reasonable? Your expectations of yourself might flow from your personal drive and need for fulfilment. There might be a legacy of parental influence or a demanding teacher. When the weight of expectation is excessive, you need to loosen yourself from this burden and reassess your key expectations.

As you think about the future it can be helpful to identify a range of possibilities rather than have too rigid an expectation about one outcome. The more you can identify two or three possible future directions, the less burdened you will feel by pursuing one particular outcome.

Mustaq's boss at his new organisation had a clear expectation that Mustaq should be promoted to lead a major engineering project. Mustaq, however, was less sure whether this was the right direction. Mustaq talked with his boss about three different possibilities, which helped him weigh up what type of expectations he was willing to commit to. Mustaq wanted to be stretched, but needed to be focused on a project that he knew was deliverable. Mustaq resisted being allocated the most controversial project, but was happy to lead on a difficult scheme that was less controversial.

In practice

- How helpful is it for you to create expectations about the future?

- When are expectations a stimulus and motivator, and when do they become a burden that saps your energy?

- How best do you balance stretching expectations with being realistic about what is possible?

- How do you react when your expectations need to be revised?

KEEP FOLLOWING YOUR DREAM

Whatever the bumps and disappointments, stay focused on your dream and how best you can follow that dream.

The idea

You might want to be the best possible schoolteacher, university lecturer, medical consultant, engineer, manager, church minister or civil servant. But something might have gone badly wrong under your watch, and you feel a strong sense of responsibility and disappointment. At low moments you are racked by a sense of failure. You are at risk of beating yourself up, when in reality you carry only part of the responsibility. You can feel gripped by the burden of having let others down. You are unsure whether you want to continue to follow the dream you had embarked upon.

You can take courage from the example of athletes who are constantly challenged by their rivals. They can either give up, or regroup and enter subsequent races with a renewed focus. Athletes continue to develop their technique and approach, learning more from failure than success.

Sometimes you should reassess whether the dream or goal you are working towards continues to be realistic. We need the perspective of others to help decide what is potentially attainable. You need to judge when to keep following a dream, and when to recalibrate and turn your attention elsewhere. It is worth periodically identifying what was the sense of vocation or dream that helped push you forward. Hold on to your dreams for the future; but also be willing to revise those dreams while watching out you don't revise those dreams prematurely. The Olympic athlete may be losing races, but can still dream of what might be possible at the next Olympic Games.[32]

Mustaq had always dreamt that one of the projects he was leading might win an award, but saw this prospect as an unrealistic dream. When his boss suggested that one of Mustaq's projects should be put forward for an award, he was initially sceptical. Mustaq told himself that he needed to test out this dream and agreed to the project being submitted. Mustaq kept telling himself that an award was unlikely, but was intrigued by this possibility. When the project received a bronze award, he was delighted.

In practice

- In respect to your leadership aims, what is the dream that you need to hold on to?

- How best do you test the reality of your dreams?

- What dreams about the future do you need to update in the light of your experience and the changing context?

---

32 See *Wake up and Dream*. Norwich: Canterbury Press.

SECTION H
BE

71 SELF-AWARE

THE MORE SELF-AWARE YOU are, the better you can anticipate your impact on others and your reactions in different situations.

The idea

In order to be single-minded in reaching desired outcomes, we can become so blinkered that our self-awareness is constrained. On other occasions our self-awareness can be so acute that we freeze and become inhibited from taking necessary action. The dial on the self-awareness button needs to be constantly adjusted so that we are fully aware of our impact on others and their impact on us— but without self-awareness stopping us doing the right thing in a particular situation.

Awareness of your impact on others comes through recognising previous patterns and understanding the personalities of those you are engaged with. Self-awareness comes from recognising your personality traits and preferences alongside an understanding of how different people and situations impact upon you. Psychometric assessments, such as the Myers-Briggs test, can be helpful in understanding personal preferences.

Systematic feedback from others can be valuable, provided it is recognised that this feedback says as much about the person giving it as it does about the individual being commented upon. It is important to ensure that self-awareness does not inhibit taking bold action. If you need to give a difficult message to someone, your awareness that it will not be well received will help you decided how to communicate this message; but this should not put a constraint on the need to deliver that message. When you sense that too much self-awareness is inhibiting you from taking necessary action, it is helpful to ask what is holding you back from taking the necessary next steps.

Andrew was conscious that giving a clear message to a colleague about their performance would be painful, both for that individual and for himself. Andrew recognised that he needed to anticipate how difficult the conversation would be and was prepared for a negative, emotional reaction from Ben. Andrew played through in his own mind the different, likely stages in the conversation and prepared himself accordingly. He knew that he had to hold his nerve and come through his own pain barrier.

In practice

- Recognise when your emotional reactions provide insights and when they might inhibit action.

- Seek to increase your levels of self-awareness through feedback from others.

- Understand your likely patterns of response in different situations.

- Know how to stop your self-awareness from inhibiting necessary action.

- Keep fine-tuning your self-awareness in new situations.

72 FOCUSED

THE KEY TO SUCCESS is to be focused and then ensure the focus is maintained—even when there is a lot of extraneous noise.

The idea

Being able to keep your focus is crucial in moving from ideas to implementation. When I write a book I set aside days when I can focus exclusively on writing chapters, and give myself a target about the number of chapters I will write each day. I seek to keep that focus both through a clear timetable and through giving myself regular, short breaks to rest my brain, before refocusing on the next section.

Being focused is not about being utterly relentless in pursuing an outcome for 100 percent of the time. The good athlete learns how to relax their muscles, then focus entirely on the race. The athlete plans the race carefully, executes precisely and then moves into a slower physical and mental pace for the post-race warm-down.

The ability to focus on the main task of the moment is a talent that is well worth cultivating. The focus might be on one person, or one calculation, or one project. The ability to focus relentlessly on one outcome over a short period ensures that mental and emotional energy is not dissipated. We can train ourselves to be increasingly focused in the way we prepare for interactions through reinforcing in our hearts and minds actions and approaches that have worked well before and that will be valuable in the future.

Effective focus is both about the short and long term. It involves a combination of being focused in the moment on the next steps, while ensuring that you keep calibrating whether your immediate focus will lead to the type of outcomes that you desire in the longer term.

Andrew knew that he had to keep focused on the key issues in the performance conversation with Ben. He prepared carefully, noting the points he needed to make in two important areas. Andrew recognised that he needed to listen to Ben's comments and concerns, and demonstrate that he was listening. Andrew knew that he must not become diverted from focusing on the messages that needed to be given to Ben, and communicate the agreed next actions.

In practice

Keep practicing the art of focusing on one issue for a half-hour period.

Recognise the type of distractions that can impede that focus and know how you counteract those distractions.

Know what 'warming down' activity you need to put in place after each period of intense focus.

Recognise how you best create a range of different types of focused activity in order to keep yourself fresh and alert.

73 ADAPTABLE

THERE ARE MOMENTS WHEN it is right to be adaptable to take account of changed circumstances or the views of key individuals or groups.

The idea

You may be entirely focused on a particular outcome, but you are conscious that some key individuals are unsure about whether it is deliverable. Your first reaction is to keep going and 'plough on regardless'. But you sense that such individuals could block your way or influence others in a different direction. Their reservations might also include some valid points.

You feel you need to listen carefully to these concerns but do not want to dilute your focus. You recognise that you need to listen dispassionately to their comments and then assess what is the best way forward, particularly if you are going to need their support. There are moments when it is right to be relentlessly focused on your original plan. There are also times when it is expedient to adapt your approach to take account of the points made by others. At the very least it is a matter of adapting your approach in order to neutralize the strength of the reservations of others.

When you are about to adapt your plan or approach, it is worth asking yourself why you are being adaptable. Is it because valid points have been raised by others, or is it necessary to find a way forward that has the endorsement of a wide range of people and perspectives? Or are you minded to be adaptable because you want to avoid a difficult conversation or wider conflict? It is important to be honest with yourself about your reasons for being adaptable.

When you do adapt, it is important to explain the reasons for your changed approach to those closest to you. Members of your team might interpret your adaptability as a lack of courage, or a limited commitment in supporting what they have been doing. Being explicit to your supporters about why you are being adaptable both forces you to crystallize your reasoning as well as helping clarifying your decision to those closest to you.

When Andrew prepared for his conversation with Ben, he had a clear timetable in mind about when certain pieces of work needed to be completed. When Ben highlighted some of the complications with the proposed timetable, Andrew's initial reaction was to stick rigidly to his original plan. But Andrew soon recognised that Ben had made some good points and concluded that he should be adaptable in agreeing a revised timetable. An agreed timescale was more likely to get Ben's full commitment than one imposed by Andrew.

In practice

- See adaptability as a strength rather than a weakness.

- When you are minded to be adaptable, be clear why. Is it for a practical reason, or is it because you are avoiding conflict?

- Be clear to yourself about the limits of your adaptability if you are to achieve your primary focus.

- Be clear in communicating why you are being adaptable.

74

THOUGHTFUL

THE MORE THOUGHTFUL WE are (and appear to be), the more engaged others will be with us.

The idea

You may think that if you appear thoughtful you will come over as hesitant and unsure of yourself. Being thoughtful is the best way of ensuring good-quality interaction with those people you need to engage with, as it involves seeking to understand fully the point of view of others. It includes wanting to hear the latest evidence and taking that carefully into your thought processes.

Being thoughtful involves seeking out people with different views and talking openly with them about the reasons for their different perspective. It includes giving credence to different perspectives and seeking to work through the implications of different courses of action. It might include identifying the factors why someone else's point of view is misconceived, and then communicating those reasons in a way that engages and does not transmit a sense of disdain or thoughtlessness.

Being thoughtful, and being seen to be thoughtful, may involve setting up different types of discussion, where some conversations encourage the interplay of a variety of views without a predetermined set of outcomes. Signalling to participants the type of conversation you are envisaging will help them come prepared—whether it is an occasion to explore in an open and thoughtful way a variety of options, or whether it is taking forward next steps on the implications of a pre-set course.

When I write a book I have a clear plan, and write each chapter to a pre-set agenda; but in the moment, I need to be continually thoughtful about how the text is going to be received. I am in a process of continuous, virtual dialogue with the reader, so I need to be regularly thinking through how to engage with the reader and how they are likely to respond.[33]

Andrew knew that in his conversations with Ben, he needed to come over as being thoughtful, to demonstrate that he was listening to the points made by Ben. Andrew deliberately left quiet moments in their conversations to allow both Ben and himself to be thoughtful. He tried to create a situation whereby both he and Ben were being reflective about the same issue, namely, to improve Ben's performance in certain areas. It was as if they were sat on the same side of the table exploring this issue, rather than being in a conflictual mode. Seeking to be thoughtful helped create the right dynamics for a constructive conversation.

In practice

- Recognise what helps you think through an issue carefully and systematically.

- Allow yourself time and space to be thoughtful about an issue; see this as a strength and not a weakness.

- Practice different ways of sharing your thoughts with others in order to create engaged conversations.

- Recognise when going into thoughtful mode might be holding you back from useful action.

---

33 See *Mirroring Jesus as Leader.* Cambridge: Grove.

75 DECISIVE

A KEY TEST FOR any leader is: can I be decisive when I need to be? And can I enable others to be decisive?

The idea

An inevitable part of leading well involves making good decisions. Sometimes the decision is yours alone to take. You have to decide whether someone is appointed to a role. You have to decide on whether a contract is agreed or ended. In most cases there is the opportunity to talk to others so that our decisions are informed by the best possible evidence and by the views of people you trust.

Most decisions, if they are going to stick, will have followed conversations with significant others to canvass their views. This can sometimes feel like a tiresome and time-consuming burden, but when people have contributed to a decision they are much more likely to be committed to ensuring its effective implementation.

Often, it is helpful to break down a big decision into a sequence of component parts whereby you are making a decision a step at a time. It is always helpful to think through the implications of different decisions and to reflect on the interplay between them. Decision-making will sometimes involve starting from total clarity about the facts. On other occasions you will have a conviction about the right way to go and when you need to test out those convictions alongside the evidence. In any decision-making process you are balancing clarity and conviction, and then having the courage to take forward decisions and communicate them effectively.

An important skill is knowing when to be decisive and how best to explain the reasons for your decision. It can be helpful to specify in advance when you are going to do this so others have an opportunity to contribute. The moment of decision requires a courageous stepping forward alongside clear communication.[34]

Andrew recognised that there was a risk that his performance conversation with Ben could go round the same points over an extended period. Andrew signalled 15 minutes before the conversation was due to end that they needed to turn to the next steps. Andrew invited Ben to set out his conclusions about next actions. Andrew was willing to be decisive about what should be achieved by when: he set this out in a way that took careful account of what Ben had said. Andrew recognised that he had to be clear and decisive about the timetable, both orally and in a follow-up note.

In practice

- Recognise what holds you back from making decisions and know how you handle those inhibitions.

- Accept that you need to balance clarity and conviction alongside being courageous and communicating decisions effectively.

- Think through who you need to involve before making a decision, and how best you engage them constructively.

- Always leave enough time and energy to communicate your decisions, while clearly recognising others' viewpoints.

---

34 See *Making Difficult Decisions: how to be decisive and get the business done*. Chichester, Capstone.

CONSIDERATE

However much you disagree with someone or have a difficult message to offer, always be considerate, as they are a human being with their own feelings, hopes and fears.

The idea

Courtesy and kindness are virtues that are always relevant. However much you feel that someone has let you down, or however much you disagree with them, demonstrating that you recognise them as a human being with emotions is important. This is partially to acknowledge the human values that are most important to you, but also because others are likely to mirror your behaviour in the long term.

Being considerate recognises the varied pressures that an individual is facing, and enables you to decide the extent to which you want to take those factors into account. You may decide that there are limits to how considerate you intend to be, if being very considerate to one person puts unreasonable pressures on other members of a team. If someone's domestic circumstances mean they need to leave work at 4:00 p.m. for two days a week, it is right to factor that into account when building a consensus with other members of the team. You might want to encourage team members to be considerate to each other in ways that take account of their own individual needs and are consistent with how the team is going to work together effectively, especially in busy periods.

Being considerate is not about following the whims of individuals in a way that can be disruptive. It involves finding a way forward that recognises the pressures on someone over a particular period, and enables them to play their full part in the team over the longer term.

Being considerate in the way you structure work will help develop the motivation and commitment of those working with you. I have worked with a number of leaders in job share arrangements that have functioned exceptionally well because of the planning and practical consideration shown between the job sharers and with the boss. It is always worth seeking to understand the personal circumstances of individuals, and how best the work pattern can take account of those circumstances, without diluting an individual's contribution to the team or organisation.

Ben explained in his conversation with Andrew that his performance had been affected by the illness of one of his children. Andrew was sympathetic and enquired how the family situation was likely to develop over the coming months. Ben thought he would continue to need some flexibility in managing his time, but did not anticipate that his family circumstances would detrimentally affect what he was able to deliver in the role. Andrew was clear that he needed to assess Ben's performance against the required criteria for the role, but wanted to provide as much flexibility as possible about how he organised his work.

In practice

- Always treat others as human beings, however disappointed or cross you are with them.

- Understand people's personal circumstances, and be considerate in how you respond to constraints that personal circumstances can put on others.

- Be mindful if you think others are taking advantage of your willingness to be considerate.

- Be aware how being considerate to one person can put unfair burdens on others.

STRATEGIC

ALWAYS HAVE AN EYE on the bigger picture. Be wary lest the immediate drives out what is important over the longer term.

The idea

Your focus will often be on what is immediate. You have a 'to do' list that needs to be tackled. There is a risk that you address the easier or the most important issues first, with the longer-term issues having a lower priority, and perhaps never reaching the top of the 'to do' list. Success as a leader depends on both doing the urgent well, and also looking effectively to the longer term and taking into account how different, wider considerations are changing.

Being strategic involves being both ambitious and realistic. It includes being conscious of future opportunities and recognising the barriers that will need to be overcome in order to deliver on those opportunities. It includes anticipating the reactions of others and seeing whether trends are taking various interests in consistent or different directions.

It is worth being clear who you can have good quality strategic conversations with and setting aside time for those conversations. It may mean planning your diary to allocate time for longer-term conversations with colleagues. Other elements might be conversations with people in external organisations who are also thinking through longer-term issues. You will want to choose the location for those conversations carefully, so the urgent and immediate does not inhibit these conversations about future direction. Taking forward longer-term issues might be about giving yourself personal space to think these issues through, or about writing a narrative covering what your world might look like in three years' time and the potential steps to get there.

Andrew agreed with Ben that they should have a conversation about long-term aims. They agreed that this conversation would cover both longer-term changes in the work of the team, and Ben's aspirations for his own personal development. At this meeting they reflected openly on the opportunities and potential barriers for the work of the team in a couple of years' time. Andrew pressed Ben to stretch his own thinking about what type of work he wanted to be doing in three to five years' time, and how best he develop skills and experience to be able to fulfil his ambitions. The conversation prompted Andrew to develop a narrative about how best his team might grow the capabilities needed over the longer term.

In practice

- Be honest about how you use your time and what priority you give to longer-term issues.

- Recognise who helps you keep focused on the strategic and longer term and then ensure you have the right type of conversations with these individuals.

- Be disciplined in ensuring you allocate enough time to address what is strategically important going forward.

78 TRUSTWORTHY

TRUST TAKES A LONG while to build up. It can be lost in an instant.

The idea

Organisations depend on there being trust between individuals. A commitment to deliver on a responsibility is based on trust as much as formal accountabilities. Successful organisations rely on people delivering what they say they will deliver.

Trust takes time to build up, as individuals recognise the importance of clear communication with shared expectations that are mutually agreed and seen as within the bounds of reasonableness.

A trusting organisation will have its own checks and balances. There needs to be opportunities for individuals to say openly whether what they committed themselves to do is still possible. It is important that there is an openness for people to express their concerns before it is too late. There needs to be the strength of trust, which means that a problem can be exposed and explored at an early stage. Finally, there needs to be clarity about whether actions have been delivered.

There is nothing more damaging to professional relationships than a breakdown of trust. If you feel that someone has gone behind your back and been critical of you, you are going to be wary of them going forward. If someone says one thing to you and the opposite to someone else, you are likely to have a degree of suspicion about anything they say to you in the future.

Being trustworthy involves being consistent in your words and actions. It means not speaking gratuitously ill of people. It means keeping to the facts when discussing the performance of individuals and teams. Building a reputation for trust involves keeping confidences and creating a situation where people can talk openly about their aspirations, hopes and fears.

Being trustworthy does not mean accepting completely what anybody else says to you. There is always a value in triangulating different viewpoints, so you are able to assess the situation or person through different perspectives. This is not about a lack of trust, it is about recognising that people see situations through their own distinct lens—hence the importance of collecting a variety of perspectives on a particular subject before deciding whose judgement you agree with.

Andrew believed he had a good working relationship with Ben going forward. Both had outlined how they were going to work together and support each other. If Ben was going to be able to step up his performance, he needed to be able to trust that Andrew would give him feedback at key moments. Andrew needed to trust Ben to take the practical steps he had committed himself to do. In a few months' time, Andrew would triangulate with others whether the progress made by Ben was as needed.

In practice

- Start by being trusting, then keep a careful eye on whether that trust has been respected.

- Trust others in the way you would want to be trusted.

- When someone has broken your trust, be willing to name the problem and talk it through by seeking to understand what has happened.

CLEAR-HEADED

THE MORE CLEAR-HEADED WE are, the better and more prescient our words and actions will be.

The idea

We celebrate having fertile minds. Our brains are often full of different ideas. We enjoy reflecting on a range of different subjects and people, and our engagement through the internet has enriched our perspective. There are key moments when we need to clear our minds of extraneous information, where we can identify core considerations that are relevant to next steps. If we don't do this we will be pushed in multifarious directions and not bring the clarity of mind essential to make progress.

We each need to find ways that work for us in clearing our minds and allowing us to be clear-headed in how we address a particular issue. For some people, going for a brisk walk can help clarify thinking. For others, it is writing down the three or four key points that matter most, or writing down a clear narrative about our next steps. It might involve asking a colleague to be a sounding board as we articulate our suggested approach.

Being clear-headed can involve identifying what is blocking us from moving forward. It can involve inviting others to critique our vision of the way forward and being frank about the risks that might inhibit progress.

It is worth being honest about the emotional noise that can get in the way of clear-headedness. What are the anxieties or fears that can blur your thinking and distort your perspective about the right action to take?

Andrew knew that he had to think through how his team might address future priorities. He recognised that he, Ben and other team members had their preferred activities and ways of working. Andrew recognised that he needed to start from what was right for the organisation and not what was preferable for the individuals involved. Andrew needed to clear his head and focus clearly on the organisation's needs and the trends in the expectations of customers that were going to be critical as the team planned its future activities.

In practice

- Be honest with yourself about the type of emotional noise in your brain.

- Recognise when you are at your most clear-headed and ensure you use those moments productively.

- Know what activities or actions help you be clear-headed, such as going out for a walk or turning off the computer.

- Know who you can best engage in conversation in a way which will enable you to clarify your thoughts.

80 GENEROUS

BE GENEROUS IN THE way you use your time and resources, while recognising the limits of that generosity.

The idea

We all remember people who have been generous with us in terms of time, attention and advice. We treasure that generosity and are conscious how much it has influenced us. We treasure the generosity of family members and good friends, even though it is often not fully deserved.

The generosity we show to others may influence them far more than we may realise over the longer term. In 20 years' time you are more likely to be remembered by those you mentored than for any of the decisions you took. Being generous with your time might mean being willing to mentor and guide colleagues and the next generation of leaders. Rationing that generosity will often be the right thing to do. You might only be able to commit five percent of your time to mentoring others, hence the importance of rationing the use of that time so the organisation and your colleagues benefit most.

Being generous with your time does not mean taking on more things than you can deliver. If someone is asking for your advice, you may well decide that you can give them your sole, undivided attention for 15 minutes. Generosity is more about the quality of the time and commitment we give to someone rather than its quantity.

There are limits to generosity. If you are a leader in a caring profession you have to have clear boundaries beyond which you do not go. You have to ration your emotional commitment to others, especially when they put their expectations on you.

Being generous may involve giving someone the benefit of the doubt. It involves giving people two or three opportunities to learn from experience. But generosity is not about diluting your standards, values and expectations about quality. Being over-generous to some people could result in others suffering unfairly.

Andrew prided himself on his generosity in terms of time and praise, but he recognised that being over-generous in praise to someone could mean that the individual had a false perspective about their contribution and future prospects. Andrew recognised that his generosity needed to be tempered with realism: he was absolutely clear that he needed to be consistently generous in allocating time for mentoring each of his team leaders.

In practice

- Whose past generosity had a profound effect on how you lead others?

- What does it mean to combine generosity and realism?

- How best do you ration generosity and use it wisely?

- When being generous, how much does the quality of attention compare to the quantity of time you give?

SECTION I
BECOME

81 BOLDER

As your confidence grows, allow yourself to become bolder in the way you advocate particular approaches.

The idea

In the first few months in any role there is an inevitable degree of hesitancy when you make contributions. After having been in a role for six months to a year, there is a natural point of progression where you become more confident about the relevance of your thoughts and suggestions. There is, however, a risk that you may continue to hold back and do not switch to a more assertive approach. A questioning approach may have stood you in good stead in the first few months, but there can be a natural tendency to continue with the same approach when you have the experience and knowledge to be bolder in your contributions.

There are risks in being bolder, too, as others might not always agree with you. They may decide they are going to be bolder as well. You can normally tell if people are listening to you and taking you seriously through their facial expressions. If there is evidence that your bolder contributions lead to more honest and effective debate, then your boldness has been justified.

Boldness does not equate with aggression or being foolhardy. Boldness is about an attitude of mind when you have weighed up the facts and believe that you have a point of view that is justified and needs to be expressed clearly. To be bold includes being willing to disagree and not be intimidated when strong views are expressed. Boldness involves being direct, but not rude or angry. Boldness is about clarity of expression, arguing clearly and persuasively.

Being bolder includes a willingness to take bigger risks than you might have done before and not be overawed by the prospect of not fully succeeding. Being bold is about holding your nerve when you are in a minority.[35]

Helen had been a board member for six months, and had learnt a great deal from her colleagues. Even in the early weeks she surprised herself by the type of questions she was asking. Her contribution seemed to be welcomed by her colleagues, but there was still a hesitancy in her that stopped her from contributing early in discussions. Six months into the job Helen decided that she knew enough about the business to be able to intervene earlier and be bolder in her contributions. She spoke earlier in some conversations and was pleased by the type of disclosures she was able to prompt.

In practice

- Be willing to make a step-change in how bold you are in your contributions.

- Recognise that your experience is growing all the time as your knowledge of the subject improves.

- Deliberately vary your timing when making bold suggestions and observe the impact on others.

- Be ready for firm push-back and demonstrate that you enjoy the ensuing debate and are not threatened by it.

- When you have been bold, be wary of going immediately onto the defensive if your position is opposed.

---

35 See *Leading in Demanding Times*. Cambridge: Grove (co-authored with Graham Shaw).

MORE AUTHORITATIVE

Authority comes from your credibility, track record and awareness of different realities.

The idea

Our authority comes from a number of different sources, including our experience, role, demeanour and our choice of words. Where we have made constructive contributions in the past, our reputation will go before us and influence the way our contribution is viewed. Whether we represent a significant group of staff, constituents or customers, our voice will carry their authority, too.

When we have a lot of experience in a particular area, our words will be regarded as carrying authority based on the breadth of that experience. Being authoritative does not depend on harking back to what has happened, but it does mean allowing our experience to inform the type of contribution we make.

Your authority does not come from the volume of words you speak. Authority flows from focused interventions that identify key questions, considerations, or consequences. When someone makes an authoritative contribution, they may well have deliberately slowed down the flow of the conversation in order to crystallize what has been said into clear options for next steps. The most authoritative interventions combine clarity of intent with a realism about obstacles that need to be overcome.

Sometimes it is appropriate to use the authority of your position to assert a way forward. The more that authority flows from good-quality dialogue and a proper consideration of the issues, the greater the likelihood that your conclusions will carry the authority of the whole team. Being more authoritative flows from recognising the need for a clear leadership intervention that builds agreement or acceptance about next steps. The more team members can express next steps as *their* conclusions rather than *your* conclusions, the stronger your authority will become.

Helen recognised that her effectiveness on the board depended on her becoming bolder and more authoritative. Helen had the confidence of people right across the organisation. She knew what people expected about the future direction and was able to draw on a wide cross-section of views when she made contributions in the leadership team. Helen became more willing to make contributions where she drew on the views of both customers and stakeholders. Her colleagues began to recognise that she had developed an authoritative voice, both within the board and more widely in the organisation, after a remarkably short time. This was attributed to her clarity of thinking, effective preparation and her willingness to speak the truth.

In practice

- Recognise the sources of your authority.

- Be willing to draw on the full range of your experiences in your contributions and the leadership you bring.

- Use informal authority to build agreement about next steps.

- Recognise when you have formal authority in your role and be wary about using that authority too often as the rationale for getting your own way.

- Do not flaunt your authority or use it in a malign or capricious way.

83 INSIGHTFUL

BEING INSIGHTFUL IS ABOUT addressing the question, 'What is really going on?'

The idea

We can know lots of information about a particular situation, which enables us to be bold. By virtue of previous experience we can be authoritative in our contribution. The type of contribution that has the biggest impact is an insightful comment that links together different bits of information and is clear about trends and implications. The most insightful person in a meeting might be making just a few comments—but their timing, and their ability to catch the imagination of the participants, is what turns a random comment into an insightful perspective that changes the course of a conversation.

As you prepare for meetings, it is worth thinking through what kind of insight you can bring that will enable participants to see an issue in a different light or open up the possibility of a new approach.

Sometimes, when a team has built a momentum and a belief that they are on the right track, there is a need for someone to say, 'We need to stop and reflect'. You may think that participants have become blinkered and are not fully cognisant of the issues they need to address. The team may benefit from someone forcing a conversation about reality. Sometimes insightful comments are about recognising hard reality. On other occasions the most insightful comments are about opportunities that are about to open up, where the team holding its nerve going forward is key to success. Often, the most insightful interventions are counter to the primary thrust of a conversation. Insightful comments can flow from asking yourself the question, 'What is really going on here?' and then being frank about your answer. Quite often others will say that they have been thinking similar thoughts but have hesitated to express them.

When Helen became a member of the board she researched her contributions carefully and was cautious in her interventions. She recognised that she had a reputation for making insightful comments because she was good at asking 'Why?' questions. Helen wanted to ensure that the board faced up to reality and reviewed whether it was achieving its values and creating a clear match between aspiration and delivery. When preparing for board meetings, for each topic Helen would think through the progress being made and whether the perception of that progress was accurate. She prepared for meetings by thinking through the insight she wanted to bring into the conversation.

In practice

- Who do you observe making the most insightful comments and what is the nature of the comments they make?

- What type of preparation enables you to stand back and answer the question: 'What is really going on here?'

- When have colleagues remarked that you have made insightful comments and how can you build on their perspective?

RESILIENT 84

BECOMING EVER MORE RESILIENT is a prerequisite of being able to sustain leadership over an extended period.

The idea

Understanding the sources of your resilience, what recharges you and what saps your energy are vital to being able to pace yourself successfully. Guarding resilience involves recognising when uncertainty creates a sense of threat and knowing how to handle darker feelings of doubt, vulnerability or alarm. Guarding resilience includes using your emotions to assess people and situations, without becoming captive to the debilitating consequences of anger, frustration or antipathy. Being conscious of how your mind works and understanding your preferences will enable you to improve your resilience.

Looking after your physical, mental, emotional and spiritual well-being is central to ensuring resilience. It includes being aware about how you can do more of whatever gives you energy. Whatever lifts your spirits is likely to make you more open-minded to different people and their ideas. Knowing the limits of your resilience is crucial, including ensuring your reserves do not become depleted.

Resilience involves building rhythms that work for you. It includes recognising when you are at your most alert to solving problems and being aware of the consequences of doing too many things at once. It is important to know the rhythms that help you feel more in control of your own situation and creativity, and know the best ways of not becoming distracted.

Building resilience for the longer term involves creating a 'virtual circle' in which you reflect, reframe, rebalance and renew. As you reflect, you become conscious of what matters most to you. As you reframe what has happened, you are keeping open to what might be possible going forward and your ability to handle potential derailers. As you rebalance, you keep professional and focused in an evolving context. As you renew, you seek to bring a lightness of touch and build constructively for the future.[36]

Just as personal and professional pressures change over time, so do our sources of resilience. It is important to keep open to new avenues and pathways, so that our curiosity is stretched and our sources of resilience are allowed to evolve and shape over time.

Helen knew that she had to take deliberate steps to maintain her strength and energy as a board member. She carried responsibilities both for her own directorate and for the organisation as a whole. Helen did not want to let others down and knew that she could become worn out if she did not look after her physical, emotional, mental and spiritual well-being. She deliberately planned some long walks with her husband over the winter months and read historical novels to take her mind into a different place. Helen deliberately renewed a number of friendships. She went on a retreat organised by an abbot who she greatly respected.

In practice

- Be self-aware about the limits of your resilience.

- Deliberately build in rhythms that enable you to pace your energies.

- Take positive action to look after your physical, mental, emotional and spiritual well-being.

- Be willing to say no to requests that will excessively drain your energy.

---

36 See *Sustaining Leadership: renewing your strength and sparkle*. Norwich: Canterbury Press.

85 CORPORATE

BECOMING MORE CORPORATE IN your contribution will increase your influence much more than you might anticipate.

The idea

When you begin your working life your impact is based in what you do as an individual. When you are promoted your impact flows from how you enable others to manage and lead well. As you progress, your influence becomes wider than your team as a consequence of participating in discussions about the direction and policy of the whole organisation.

You may be invited to become a member of groups planning future policy, or selection panels or committees that are looking at how the organisation should change going forward. At first glance being a part of corporate activity can seem like a diversion from your day job. But the well-being of all organisations depends on the commitment of its leaders and managers to ensuring that the organisation is vibrant, healthy and forward-looking.

Playing an effective part within corporate activities will provide you with valuable development opportunities. It enables you to build links beyond your particular area and develop a wider understanding of different perspectives. It provides a good opportunity to influence and engage with colleagues who have different responsibilities and interests. Making a corporate contribution provides an excellent opportunity to learn from others and to experiment with different approaches to engaging and influencing others.

It is important to maintain a balance between a commitment to your own area of responsibility and your wider, corporate contribution, as your overall performance is likely to be assessed primarily in relation to specific areas of responsibility; but learning from one area will always feed beneficially into the other.

When Helen became a member of the board, she suddenly appreciated that her corporate responsibility meant that she needed to hold in her mind the well-being of the whole organisation. Her responsibility as a board member was primarily concern with the direction of the organisation and the quality of its work and impact. Helen was called upon to be part of a range of planning groups and to be on appointment panels. Helen gained hugely from this experience while recognising that it was often difficult to balance holding together both her individual and corporate responsibilities.

In practice

- See corporate responsibilities as an opportunity and not a burden.

- Be selective in the type of corporate responsibilities you are willing to take on.

- Be explicit about the type of influence you want to have corporately and the learning you want to gain from different, wider roles.

- Be selective in the learning you gain from corporate contributions.

ABLE TO LIVE WITH AMBIGUITY

BALANCING DIFFERENT PRIORITIES AND expectations is part of life for any leader.

The idea

Our ideal may be to have a set of straightforward priorities, with clear next steps, in each area of life. But life is rarely so straightforward. In our home lives we are balancing different expectations from our children, our partner, the wider family and our community responsibilities.

In our work, we have accountabilities to a range of different people. A senior teacher has responsibilities to pupils, parents, colleagues and the deputy head. The expectations on her may not be fully aligned. The good senior teacher is able to hold these different responsibilities together in a way that maintains equilibrium. She will never be able to satisfy all the parents all of the time. Her colleagues will not think she makes the right decisions every day. Her role requires her to recognise and live with the fact that all these expectations will not be fully aligned. Living with this level of ambiguity is inevitable.

A senior civil servant may feel a strong sense of expectation to deliver for the cabinet minister in one area and a junior minister in a different area. The civil servant recognises that they have to ensure their resources are used to deliver as effectively as possible for both ministers. There are moments when it is important to be explicit about the different priorities from the two ministers; but for most of the time, the civil servant recognises they have to deliver for both individuals, while making a judgement about how the resources of the department are apportioned effectively between priorities. It is important to be open with your boss or a trusted colleague about how best you manage competing expectations. A trusted sounding board can help you achieve an equilibrium about how best to live with ambiguity.

Helen recognised that her staff wanted her to be their representative on the board. Helen fully appreciated that her prime responsibility as a board member was about the well-being and the health of the whole organisation. Helen understood that she needed to ensure that the board was aware of the priorities and concerns of her people, and recognised that she was not on the board only as their representative. When Helen spoke at a board meeting, she was clear that she was balancing varied interests, but she did ensure that her contribution included the concerns of staff. Once she got used to her board responsibilities, Helen was comfortable with the different expectations placed upon her.

In practice

- Recognise that living with ambiguity is part of what any leader has to do.

- Accept that leadership is about finding an equilibrium between competing expectations.

- Be honest with yourself and others if conflicting expectations make your role unsustainable.

- Seek sounding boards with whom you can talk through how you live with ambiguity and different sets of expectations.

87 MORE SELF-REFERENCING

IT IS IMPORTANT TO be able to self-assess your contributions rather than being dependent upon the assessment of others.

The idea

Feedback from others is important in assessing whether you are making an appropriate contribution. Good quality feedback will always inform you, provided you collate feedback from different people so you are responding to broad themes rather than the idiosyncratic views of particular individuals.

As you progress in an organisation, you are likely to get less feedback as people will be deferential to your seniority and respectful of your role. When you take up a senior leadership position, you may become increasingly conscious that you are on your own, with your staff now being reluctant to give you any negative feedback.

The more senior you become, the greater the need to be able to self-reference and self-assess your contribution. You need to be able to judge when to intervene and how best to do so. You will be able to observe when this has worked well or less well. What matters is viewing that evidence objectively, so that you can continue to refine how you intervene and the results you want from these interventions. It can be helpful to be systematic in the way you assess your contribution by noting down impacts and whether you would use a different approach on the next occasion. It is still important to seek feedback from others, but you might focus this towards particular subjects or meetings, where you want to supplement your own self-assessment of what happened.

Helen was conscious that her staff were more reluctant to say what they thought to her directly now she was a board member. Her physical distance from her staff had increased as she was now co-located with other board members. Helen deliberately spent time sitting with her team and engaging with them—but she accepted that she needed to self-assess whether she was making the right type of contribution. Helen recognised that she needed to ask direct questions of her staff about specific meetings or subjects to get the type of feedback she wanted. Part of growing into the board-level role was developing the capacity to self-assess where she should be spending her time and establishing whether she was making the right type of impact. Helen recognised the inevitability of this development and was glad she could self-assess without too much emotional baggage getting in the way.

In practice

- How might you stand back and assess your own contributions?

- What needs to happen for you to be more confident in the judgements you make about how you spend your time?

- How best do you seek feedback in a way that supplements your own self-assessment and targets your questions of prime concern?

- What is your next step in self-assessment, and what practical approaches should you use to do this systematically?

LESS DEPENDENT ON THE APPROVAL OF OTHERS

Being less dependent on the approval of others is part of growing into full maturity as a leader.

The idea

All children know when they have the approval or not of their parents. The approval of parents reinforces the right type of behaviour, even though the toddler may appear to be fighting against these expectations. Wise parents know that as children grow up, they need to be able to have the freedom to make their own decisions and not have their wishes subjugated to the approval of their parents.

When you apply for a job you need the approval of the selection panel if you are to be appointed. In the early days in any new role the approval of your boss is fundamental to your initial success. As you progress in the role you want to ensure you have the overall approval of your boss, while not needing to seek their specific approval for each piece of work.

Initially you may feel that you need the boss's emotional approval if you are to thrive in the role. Too much focus on emotional approval can lead to an unhealthy dependency, whereby you feel inhibited from taking any decisions without the explicit and warm approval of your boss.

It can be helpful to clarify your thinking about when you need the approval of your boss and how this should be changing over time. You should be honest with yourself about how much of your need for approval is about agreement or alignment of purpose, and how much it is an emotional need. When it feels like an emotional need, it can be helpful to reflect on why that is your experience. Do you have a parent/child type relationship, where you are seeking emotional approval that can be unhealthy in a working relationship? If this happens, it is worth thinking about how you convert this into a more adult-to-adult relationship, and be less dependent on the approval of your boss.

Helen was very grateful to the chairman of the board who appointed her, and had a clear narrative in her mind about the expectations of her boss. After a few months Helen became concerned that she needed the approval of her boss too much. She was reluctant to disagree with him, even when she felt he was wrong. Helen recognised that she needed to address this issue and talked openly with her boss about this inhibition. It greatly helped that her boss responded by saying he wanted Helen to be explicit with him when she thought he was going in the wrong direction. Her boss was clear that he wanted their working relationship to be an honest, open, adult-to-adult relationship. This reassurance liberated Helen from previous inhibitions.

In practice

- Whose approval matters most to you?

- Are you over-dependent on the approval of some people?

- When is your need for approval part of the proper, formal processes and when is it about your emotional needs?

- How can you become more systematic in observing when your need for emotional approval is getting in the way?

- How can you become less dependent on the approval of others?

89   MORE COMFORTABLE IN YOUR OWN SKIN

BECOMING MORE COMFORTABLE IN your skin is about accepting who you are as a leader and being authentic in the way you lead.

The idea

We have all observed leaders who look out of place, uncomfortable and edgy in their approach. We are wary of them because they are unpredictable and often exude emotional vibes that are unsettling and unhelpful.

Most of us also know leaders who seem comfortable in their skin, who are consistent in their approach and seem unruffled by shifting expectations or the unexpected behaviours of others. We feel much more at ease with such leaders and more able to give of our best.

How best do you become comfortable in yourself as a leader? The key is in understanding what brings the best out of you and reading yourself well. Being comfortable in yourself as a leader involves knowing how you respond to disappointments and the unexpected. The successful leader sees them as part of life and essential to their learning. You should approach your own future in a candid way, where you are balancing your own drive and motivation, alongside being philosophical about what might happen.

Part of being more comfortable in your own skin as a leader is being true to who you are. This means knowing your strengths and building on them, and recognising how you handle your weaker areas. Being authentic is not pretending to be someone other than who you are. At the same time, being authentic is allowing yourself to continue to grow in confidence and authority and not letting self-limiting beliefs get in the way of progress.

It is worth asking yourself, how can I become increasingly relaxed in who I am as an individual? Central to this is being clear about the values that are most important to you and allowing those values to continue to shape the way you lead and respond to others. It can be helpful to ask yourself: in what leadership context do I feel most at home? This approach can give you valuable clues about where you are most likely to thrive.[37]

Helen was initially apprehensive about attending board meetings. As time went on she felt increasingly at home in that environment and able to speak her own mind. She felt increasingly comfortable in her own skin with her senior colleagues. This was partially because she had built thoughtful working relationships with her colleagues, but also because she felt increasingly relaxed working with her senior colleagues and operating at the board level. Helen felt she could make a useful contribution by being herself and speaking honestly and openly about her perspectives.

In practice

- In which context are you most at home in your own skin? What do you learn from this observation about how best you thrive?

- How might you become increasingly authentic, living your values in the way you lead?

- What would need to happen for you to be increasingly comfortable in your own skin in meetings where you currently feel a little ill at ease?

---

37 See *Thriving in Your Work*. Singapore: Marshall Cavendish.

90 | THE BEST VERSION OF YOURSELF

You are on a continuous journey where you are becoming either a better version of yourself, or a caricature of yourself.

The idea

At the age of 67 I have no desire to retire, as I observe that when some people retire they become caricatures of themselves, less open to change and less willing to take account of the perspective of others. Those who have moved more smoothly into this phase have seen 'retirement' as the start of their next phase of life and have taken on wider interests.

We are continually evolving as people through our family circumstances and our experiences. Becoming a parent or a grandparent provides personal fulfilment, and prompts us to move into the next phase of life, where we contribute and learn in different ways.

When someone moves into a new role, I encourage them to think through what is the best version of themselves that they want to bring to the fore. I do not encourage them to reinvent themselves in an entirely different way. Becoming the best version of yourself is not about undergoing a personality transplant; it involves recognising when you are at your best, what you do really well and how best you can use your talents in a more confident way.

It is helpful to work on how you reinforce your behaviours and approaches through your attitude, your preparation and the type of feedback and support you seek from others. The best version of yourself will be engaged, inquiring, curious and purposeful. It will encourage a forward rather than a backward momentum, recognising that your learning will be faster at certain times than others.

At every stage of life it is worth asking yourself: what am I learning, how am I embedding that learning, how am I sharing that learning with others, and how am I shaping my own attitudes and approaches in a constructive way? Continuing to be the best version of yourself will involve living with the realities of health, family circumstances, financial well-being and applying your understanding of spiritual truth. Do keep exploration going: it does not stop when you reach a particular age.

Helen had the opportunity to become a non-executive director of a different board, which gave her an opportunity to be the best version of herself in a different context. Helen was able to apply her confidence and experience from being an executive board member and learn about how to be an effective non-executive board member where the accountabilities were very different. As a non-executive member she was expected to bring a strategic approach. Her new role allowed her to define and then demonstrate the best version of herself.

In practice

- What characterises you at your best now?

- What might the best version of yourself look like in two years' time?

- What opportunities do you have to continue to develop the best version of yourself?

- How do you ensure that you are the best version of yourself as a leader more of the time?

HOW YOU ARE CHANGING

HAVING AN ACCURATE PERCEPTION about how you are changing enables you to be thoughtful and realistic about what you might do next.

The idea

Each day we are changing. We are a day older and will have had new or repeated experiences that stimulate our curiosity or reinforce previous ways of thinking. It is difficult to stand still for an extended period. Short-term respite renews our physical and emotional energy. If we stand still for too long our muscles begin to seize up and our body temperature drops.

In a work environment we are either moving forward or at risk of going backwards. If we stand still the world can be passing us by, as any organisation has to adapt and change to the context around it. If we become set in our ways and resistant to change, the sense of freshness and engagement in us diminishes. Others may be less inclined to engage with us if we are looking backwards rather than forwards. We can move from being an influential voice about the future to an irrelevant voice from the past in very quick time.

When there are young people in our lives we are conscious that we need to keep up to speed with them and their activities. Unless we keep active and fresh in our thinking, the young people in our lives will have moved on and regard us as an irrelevance and not a source of wisdom.

It is worth calibrating from time to time how your attitudes and approaches have changed and how your views have moved on. What matters to you most will still be core to your values and personality, but an honest recognition of how your preferences and attitudes have changed will enable you to stay open to new learning about yourself and how you engage with others.

During her thirties Rose had focused her energy on her growing family. She had worked part-time and done undemanding jobs. In her mid-forties, Rose successfully applied for promotion and was both delighted and apprehensive about the role she was about to embark on. Rose was conscious that some of her contemporaries had been promoted at an earlier age. She observed herself taking on the mantle of the more senior role rapidly and becoming influential. Through conversations with her coach, she recognised that she was blossoming into a leadership role through drawing on her mix of previous experience. Rose recognised that through her range of community voluntary activities and life as a parent she had learned ways of influencing others that equipped her to take on this leadership role in a confident and impressive way.

In practice

- Be honest with yourself if you feel stuck in a rut and are not developing or changing in your approach and attitudes.

- Accept that the way we develop is influenced by events and is rarely in a straight line.

- Seek to calibrate through your own assessment and the views of others how you are changing and celebrate where your confidence has grown.

WHAT WILL BRING THE BEST OUT OF YOU

Know which people and situations bring out the best in you and deliberately seek out those places and people.

The idea

Thinking through who or what will bring the best out of you is not indulgent. It is important to be realistic and honest with yourself about the type of situations and people that allow you to reflect, be curious and move on.

What brings out the best in me as a coach is thinking into the heart and mind of my coachee and preparing two or three key areas for exploration. This short process before I meet an individual enables me to be fully focused and gauge how best I might engage with them.

Managing the barometer of your energy helps put you into a frame of mind where you can be at your best. If you want to give your best to others, being deliberate in how you renew your energy is critical. Creating space for rest and reflection provides moments of renewal so that you can be at your most engaged.

It is worth clearly exploring which conversations bring the best out in you. Who lifts your spirits through banter or the exchange of a smile or anecdote? Who do you converse with who raises your curiosity and motivation? When you have a difficult problem that you can't easily answer, with whom can you talk the issues through in an open way that can help you turn a problem into an opportunity? Whose very presence makes you feel good about yourself and more engaged with the future and optimistic about what might be possible?

Rose reflected that the two people who brought the best out in her were her new boss and her ten-year-old son. Her new boss recognised Rose's gifts and gave her lots of opportunities to shine and focused, constructive feedback. Rose knew her boss was committed to her success and would be there for advice and support whenever Rose needed this. Rose's ten-year-old son brought out the best in her because they enjoyed their activities together with lots of laughter. Their conversations were fun as they explored ideas and possibilities together. Rose was delighted that two different people in different spheres were there for her.

In practice

- Be deliberate about spending time with the people who enable you to feel positive about life.

- Take delight in people in very different spheres with whom you can smile and laugh and who encourage you.

- Recognise when you have put off for too long spending time with people who bring the positive in you to the fore.

- Keep affirming those people who bring the best out of you and let the joy of engagement with them linger in your heart and mind.

WHERE YOU MIGHT FALL OVER

IT IS HELPFUL TO be honest about where you might fall over and your limitations going forward, without this inhibiting you too much.

The idea

I am very happy to carry my young grandchild in a backpack on an even path. But I am reluctant to have the responsibility of a grandchild on my back walking over rough ground or up steep paths. My fear is that with the additional weight on my back I might fall over or slip, resulting in injury to this young life. In some ways I feel I am letting the parents down by taking limited shifts in carrying the weight of a grandchild, but realism and a sense of caution kick in when thinking about the child's well-being. I am not worried about myself falling over on a slippery path during a long-distance walk, but I do not want to fall over and hurt someone else.

It is right to be continually reflecting on how you can keep extending your repertoire and pushing the boundaries about what is possible. On the other hand, a realistic view of our limitations and where we might fall over is necessary for our well-being and credibility. If there is a danger that you could lose your cool with some people or in some contexts, be mindful of that risk and maintain a proper degree of caution. When there is a risk of you losing your cool, it is right to prepare for that eventuality and think through how you would extricate yourself, albeit temporarily, from a situation where your approach and behaviour could be damaging or below your best.

Being honest about your limitations might lead you to want to address them (e.g., becoming better at public speaking), or circumvent them (e.g., by defining your role in relation to your strengths and building a team which complements your strengths). Some of your limitations might flow from your age or time constraints. Central to moving on is recognising which limitations you have to live with and accept, and which can be modified over time.

Rose was conscious that she did not react well to aggressive behaviour. In such situations she tended to withdraw or become apologetic. Rose recognised that these were not always the best responses. She was deliberate in observing how others handled aggressive behaviour. She recognised that sometimes she needed to withdraw for a period to clarify her approach, and then re-enter the working relationship with a new resolve. Rose recognised that there would always be in her a vulnerability in how she responded to criticism, but she was clear she did not want this to be a limitation on her aspirations for the future.

In practice

- Be honest with yourself about where you might fall over or let yourself down.

- Be deliberate about planning to minimise the chances of falling over and letting yourself down.

- Where you feel you have on-going limitations, think through how you work cooperatively with others so your limitations do not get in the way.

94 HOW YOU MIGHT EXPLORE YOUR OWN FUTURE

IF YOU ARE CONFIDENT about the questions that are most important to you, you are much more likely to explore your future in a constructive way.

The idea

When I coach people who are thinking about their own future, I encourage them to consider different options. What will give them joy and fulfilment over the next few years? What is the sense of vocation for them or sense of purpose that might blossom in the next phase of their life?

In the later part of my first career in government my son, Graham, pressed me to 'pretend you are 21 again'. These words rang in my ears and helped me think positively about my own future. This phrase enabled me to link together aspirations from when I was 21 into thoughts about what might be possible going forward aged 55. Graham's words were cathartic in helping me recognise how much I enjoyed working with individuals and teams, which then led to a second, very fulfilling career coaching individuals and teams.

As adults we are supposed to have found our future and be living it, but life does not always work like that. We may encounter false starts and dead-ends, and become bored, frustrated or downhearted. There are times when we need to be looking for new beginnings and be ready to discover new qualities in ourselves, whatever life may throw at us.

The fast-moving changes in the economy, technology and society mean we need to keep finding our future and move into different situations at different ages. The belief that there are always new beginnings can keep us seeking opportunities. We may be less active, but might have more time available in our sixties and seventies. What is important is having the desire to explore different possibilities into the future and engagement with others with whom we can talk through different avenues. We need people who believe in us who can affirm, challenge and encourage us as we think through the next steps on our leadership journey.[38]

Rose enjoyed the responsibilities in her current role and could happily continuing doing it for years ahead, but she recognised that in her organisation there was an assumption that managers moved every three to five years. She had to be realistic about this expectation and began to think about future options. When Rose felt apprehensive about whether she could master future difficult roles, she reminded herself that taking on her current role had helped create a step-change in her confidence and influence. Whatever her next role, if Rose chose carefully, it would further reinforce the contribution she was able to bring to her workplace.

In practice

- Be willing to explore the potential level of joy and fulfilment in different, future options.

- See moving on as an inevitability that will open up possibilities and not be something to dread.

- Be mindful about the values you want to be central in whatever you do next.

- See a future that includes opportunities and not just fears.

---

38 See *Finding Your Future: the second time around*. London, Darton Longman and Todd.

WHO ARE THE COMPANIONS YOU NEED TO TREASURE

KNOWING WHO IS WALKING alongside you helps you keep your resolve and recognise where you are heading.

The idea

For the last nine years Frances and I have walked with the same group during May on different long-distance walks in northern England. There has been a strong sense of companionship and mutual support on these walks, with a sharing of experiences and views. We keep each other motivated on the climbs and share stories in the evening. The sense of companionship keeps us motivated when walking through wind and rain.

There will have been companions who have been important to you in your work. You have walked with them for a period and then moved into a different sphere. Some of our companions may be for a season, when a particular task needs to be accomplished. We walk with some colleagues over a longer period, working more or less closely with them during different phases.

We will have got to know some colleagues more closely, who become sources of encouragement through difficult patches. They are the sort of work companions with whom we can talk through difficult things, in the knowledge that they will not think the worst of us or seek to undermine us.

There may be four or five people with whom you have shared a similar leadership journey who you can reconnect with quickly and whose perspective continues to be helpful, even though you are now in different spheres. Your attachment to such companions is partly through intellectual rapport and partly an emotional alliance. Such a shared journey can reinforce the bonds of companionship as you enter the next phase of your leadership journey, provided there is an openness about what you are experiencing and a willingness to take feedback from them.

Rose had built a strong rapport with three other women who were balancing work with family priorities. Rose felt that they were companions on similar journeys with whom she could be frank about frustrations and celebrate the delight of making progress in her chosen career. Some of her work companions from an earlier part of her career were now in very different spheres, and contact with them was limited. But with these three ladies, Rose knew that there was a strong degree of attachment and support that was going to be mutually important over the next few years.

In practice

- Who are the work companions who are most important to you?

- How do you nurture that companionship so that it is honest, constructive and supportive over the years ahead?

- How might you affirm how much you appreciate those who are companions on a similar journey?

WHAT WILL GIVE YOU GREATEST JOY

Being clear what gives you greatest joy helps shape how you want to use your time and energy in the way you lead.

The idea

In the latter part of my career as a Director General in the UK Government, what gave me greatest joy was developing the next generation of leaders. Working closely with government ministers was giving me less fulfilment than it had at earlier stages in my career. Seeking to build on what gave me fulfilment and joy provided me with the motivation to develop a second career in coaching, writing and teaching. After 13 years coaching and writing, I continue to delight in the joy I receive in working with individuals and teams.

In my coaching work I often ask people, 'What is giving you joy in your work and what might give you joy in the future?' I work on the basis that if you are experiencing joy you are much more likely to be motivated, energetic and successful. Not every task is joyful: having a difficult performance conversation or giving a difficult message to a customer is not joyful. But overall, does the combination of influencing and leading others lift your spirits and give you a deep sense of joy and fulfilment, or do you feel flat and exhausted?

When the joy goes out of our work, it might be time to take a hard look at whether we are focusing on the right activities in the most productive way. Sometimes the joy element is not part of your leadership experience because you and your organisation are going through tough times. It is a matter of recognising this reality and focusing on where you can make a worthwhile contribution.

Rose recognised that she needed to restructure the organisation she led. Difficult problems needed to be addressed and not deferred. She accepted that tough decisions were needed, but that the decisions would not be straightforward. She wanted to ensure the strength of the organisation, but there would be pain in the process. Those who would have to leave the organisation would not thank her for her action. Rose held in her mind the type of buoyant organisation she wanted to create, where joy would be a characteristic. This helped her work through the pain barrier over this next, tough period.

In practice

- As a leader, how best do you define joy?

- What enables you to be at your most joyful and fulfilled as a leader?

- How best do you hold in your mind future joy and fulfilment at times when the leadership experience is tough, painful and unrelenting?

WHAT IS THE NEW LIFE YOU WANT TO CREATE FOR OTHERS

CREATING NEW LIFE AND hope for others can be part of your personal fulfilment and legacy.

The idea

What is important for me as I move into the next phases of my life is to continue the journey with my children, their spouses and our grandchildren. It has been a special delight for Frances and me that our fourth grandchild spent the first six months of his life living in our home, as our daughter and son-in-law's home was being refurbished. Seeing new life at first hand is so special (especially when you can hand back the crying baby to his parents).

When you lead others, you create an environment where there can be new life and hope. The lead you give can create an atmosphere where people are hopeful and forward looking, or dejected and backward looking. The seed has to die before there can be new life. Physical birth is painful. The birth of new life in organisations is hugely demanding and exhausting, but always worthwhile.

Part of our responsibility as leaders is to create a culture where there can be hope and new life. There are younger people who you can equip and inspire, so that they move into leadership responsibilities in a way that develops their capabilities and confidence to the full. The values you live by and the tone you set will rub off on them. Your influence may well extend far beyond the period when you held a leadership role. When you have helped someone break out of a set of self-limiting beliefs you can enjoy observing their liberation and leadership journey from a distance. Be thankful for those opportunities to influence and nurture a subsequent generation.

Rose delighted in enabling the younger leaders who worked for her to take on leadership responsibilities and lead at different events. She helped a couple of people returning from career breaks to regain their confidence quickly. She was able to assist a couple of her team leaders and reassure them when projects they were involved in went wrong. She helped them work through the implications of their learning so that they were not scarred by the experience and were better equipped for future, similar eventualities.

In practice

- Remember who helped you become renewed when you were dispirited and give thanks for their effect on you.

- Identify when those you lead look dejected and reflect on how you can give them hope going forward.

- Think through how you might create situations where the next generation of leaders can benefit from the experience of others.

THE UNAVOIDABLE REALITIES IN YOUR PERSONAL WORLD

RECOGNISING AND LIVING WITH unavoidable realities gives you a platform to think creatively about your own future contribution.

The idea

Fighting against your personal realities is unlikely to be helpful. The reality might be a painful childhood, difficult family relationships, physical or emotional health issues, or a legacy of previous bad decisions. Our circumstances are what they are, however they came about. There is a physical, emotional, cultural and economic reality that underpins all our lives.

Accepting unavoidable realities does not mean giving up hope for the future or accepting second best. It does involve recalibrating what is doable and sustainable. Where there is a reality of physical or emotional pain, how best do we live with that inevitability and turn it into a new way of thinking about the future?

I recently worked with someone who was under strict instructions to work only five hours a day for a six month period for health reasons. This constraint forced this individual to restructure how they spent their time and how they best applied their leadership role when they were based largely at home. Living with this unavoidable reality required this individual to change the way she worked to ensure it could be sustained. The long-term effect was a fundamental shift in the way she worked, which she now views as a positive outcome of working through a health issue.

The more you can accept unavoidable realities in constraining your freedom, the better you are able to respond constructively without feeling that the opportunity to lead and influence is coming to a devastating conclusion.

When Rose's husband, Stephen, lost his job, she immediately recognised that there would be less household income and she would be having to deal with a grumpy spouse. She reminded herself how much she enjoyed her role and had been pleased to be promoted, both because of the job interest and the additional income that this brought into the household. The reality going forward was that Stephen might not get another job that paid as well as his former employment. What mattered would be Stephen finding work that would engage him and provide the flexibility to enable his continued involvement with responsibilities for the children.

The reality for Rose was that she would become the main source of household income. She would feel less inhibited about seeking further promotions, as there was likely to be more flexibility at home and the extra income would be useful. There were pluses, too, for Stephen, who had the opportunity to focus on getting fitter and be more involved in the community.

In practice

- What are the unavoidable realities in your personal world that limit what you can do as a leader?

- How best do you view those personal realities as part of the tapestry of life rather than a tedious limitation?

- How might working through unavoidable realities help you develop a more sustainable way of leading well and managing the way you influence others?

WHAT MIGHT BE THE DEFINING MOMENTS FOR YOU GOING FORWARD

IT CAN HELP US think constructively about the future if we can anticipate defining moments that are going to be important to us.

The idea

A defining moment you might be looking forward to could be the birth of your first child or grandchild, your next promotion, or your retirement. A defining moment might be an event that gives you special pleasure, or it might be a new insight or understanding about your future contribution. When you climb a hill in the Lake District, a defining moment might be the last steps before you reach the summit, or it might be the moment you see a vista of other mountains and lakes. It can be helpful to view some defining moments as making progress, while other defining moments are when our eyes are opened to life's possibilities.

Perhaps there is a defining moment when you recognise that you are not going to move up the greasy ladder of ambition. Instead of looking relentlessly upwards, you are now looking outwards to see what opportunities you can embrace in a different sphere. It was a defining moment for me when I got my third rejection following interviews for university vice chancellor roles. I stopped trying to push a door that would not open and decided to take forward coaching, which proved to be a wonderfully fulfilling, sideways step.

A defining moment can be a 'no' as much as a 'yes'. If we accept that defining moments might change our lives in ways that we had not initially hoped or expected, then we can be open-minded to travelling a different route and not being bound by preconceived notions of success.

Rose became an ambassador for the organisation where she worked, speaking on its behalf in front of critical audiences. She recognised that it would be a defining moment for her when she had to contend with public criticism. Rose was surprised that she was able to handle conflict situations with more equanimity than she had anticipated. Perhaps she was tougher than she thought: she recognised that if she believed in the case she was arguing and had robust evidence, then she could handle whatever was thrown at her. This gave her a new insight into herself and a new level of courage that she had not previously thought was there.

In practice

- How open are you to defining moments that could lead to a fundamental shift in the way you think and act?

- How open are you to engineering defining moments that are outside your comfort zone?

- How ready are you, when a defining moment is a resounding 'no', to be open to switching direction, learning new insights and accepting new uncertainties?

WHAT ARE THE BELIEFS AND ATTITUDES THAT ARE FUNDAMENTAL TO YOUR NEXT STEPS

CONSTANTLY RETURNING TO YOUR core beliefs and values provides you with a rationale and a sense of purpose that equips you for your leadership journey ahead.

The idea

Your beliefs and values are the bedrock of who you are and how you lead. For most leaders, their beliefs and values are explicit and recognised by themselves and others. Some leaders might not articulate their beliefs and values, but their attitudes and decisions will flow from their clear sense of what good leadership is.

Where there is a belief that there can be new life and hope, this influences how we lead. If you believe that forgiveness and reconciliation are necessary for human communities to thrive, then you will find yourself forgiving and building reconciliation. If you believe that all human beings have strengths and gifts that need to be developed and deployed, your natural approach will be to want to help people grow and bring the best out of them.

It is helpful, periodically, to do a personal stocktake about how your beliefs have been influencing the way you lead, and whether the values you seek to live by are obvious to others. It can be useful to consult a coach or mentor about the beliefs and values that are going to help shape your sense of vocation and purpose over the next few years. A key test of maturing leadership is how we apply our values to the realities we face, and then be consistent in the messages we tell ourselves and the leadership we bring to others.

Rose wanted to make a difference in the way she led. She wanted to lead in a way which valued people, while recognising that this sometimes meant giving people hard messages. She cared very much for her family, her staff and the people the organisation was serving. Rose also recognised that she needed to care for herself so that she did not become exhausted and thereby limit the contribution she could make. Every six months, Rose returned to review a note she had written to herself when she was first promoted that outlined the beliefs and values that were most important to her in her work. This refreshed and renewed her, allowing her to hold her head up high, however many responsibilities she was balancing.

In practice

- What are the beliefs and values which underlie your current leadership role and where are they leading to in terms of your aspirations at work, in the community and with your family?

- In what ways are those beliefs and values evolving in the light of experience?

- What beliefs and values are unchanged and continue to frame the way you lead?

BOOKS BY DR PETER SHAW

Mirroring Jesus as Leader. Cambridge: Grove, 2004.

Conversation Matters: how to engage effectively with one another. London: Continuum, 2005.

The Four Vs of Leadership: vision, values, value-added and vitality. Chichester: Capstone, 2006.

Finding Your Future: the second time around. London: Darton, Longman and Todd, 2006.

Business Coaching: achieving practical results through effective engagement. Chichester: Capstone, 2007 (co-authored with Robin Linnecar).

Making Difficult Decisions: how to be decisive and get the business done. Chichester: Capstone, 2008.

Deciding Well: a Christian perspective on making decisions as a leader. Vancouver: Regent College Publishing, 2009.

Raise Your Game: how to succeed at work. Chichester: Capstone, 2009.

Effective Christian Leaders in the Global Workplace. Colorado Springs: Authentic/Paternoster, 2010.

Defining Moments: navigating through business and organisational life. Basingstoke: Palgrave Macmillan, 2010.

The Reflective Leader: standing still to move forward. Norwich: Canterbury Press, 2011 (co-authored with Alan Smith).

Thriving in Your Work: how to be motivated and do well in challenging times. Singapore: Marshall Cavendish, 2011.

Getting the Balance Right: leading and managing well. Singapore: Marshall Cavendish, 2013.

Leading in Demanding Times. Cambridge: Grove, 2013 (co-authored with Graham Shaw).

The Emerging Leader: stepping up in leadership. Norwich: Canterbury Press, 2013 (co-authored with Colin Shaw).

100 Great Personal Impact Ideas. Singapore: Marshall Cavendish, 2013.

100 Great Coaching Ideas. Singapore: Marshall Cavendish 2014.

Celebrating Your Senses. Delhi: ISPCK, 2014.

Sustaining Leadership: renewing your strength and sparkle. Norwich: Canterbury Press, 2014.

100 Great Team Effectiveness Ideas. Singapore: Marshall Cavendish, 2015.

Wake Up and Dream: stepping into your future. Norwich: Canterbury Press, 2015.

100 Great Building Success Ideas. Singapore: Marshall Cavendish, 2016.

The Reluctant Leader: coming out of the shadows. Norwich: Canterbury Press, 2016 (co-authored with Hilary Douglas).

FORTHCOMING BOOKS

Living with Never-ending Expectations. Cambridge: Grove, 2017.

100 Great Leading Through Rapid Change Ideas. Singapore: Marshall Cavendish, 2018.

BOOKLETS

Riding the Rapids. London: Praesta, 2008 (co-authored with Jane Stephens).

Seizing the Future. London: Praesta, 2010 (co-authored with Robin Hindle-Fisher).

Living Leadership: finding equilibrium. London: Praesta, 2011.

The Age of Agility. London: Praesta, 2012 (co-authored with Steve Wigzell).

Knowing the Score. London: Praesta, 2016 (co-authored with Ken Thompson).

Copies of the above booklets can be downloaded from the Praesta website (www.praesta.co.uk).

ABOUT THE AUTHOR

Peter Shaw works with individuals, teams and groups to help them grow their strengths and tackle demanding issues confidently. His objective is to help individuals and teams to clarify the vision of what they want to be, the values that are driving them, the value-added they want to bring and their sources of vitality.

His work on how leaders step up successfully into demanding leadership roles and sustain that success was recognised with the award of a Doctorate by Publication from the University of Chester in 2011.

Peter was a founding partner of Praesta Partners, an international specialist coaching business. His clients enjoy frank, challenging conversations leading to fresh thinking and new insights. It is the dynamic nature of the conversations that provide a stimulus for creating reflection and new action. He often works with chief executives and board members, taking on new roles and leading major organisational change. Peter has worked with a wide range of different leadership teams as they tackle new challenges.

Peter has worked with chief executives and senior teams in a range of different sectors and countries across six continents. He has led workshops on such themes as 'Riding the Rapids', 'Seizing the Future', 'Thriving in your Work', 'Being an Agile Leader' and 'Building Resilience'.

Peter has held a wide range of board-level posts covering finance, personnel, policy, communications and delivery. He has worked in five UK government departments (Treasury, Education, Employment, Environment and Transport). He delivered major, national changes such as radically different pay arrangements for teachers, a huge expansion in nursery education and employment initiatives that helped bring UK unemployment below a million.

He led the work on the merger of the UK Government Departments of Education and Employment. As finance director general, he managed a £40bn budget and introduced radical changes in funding and accountability arrangements. In three director general posts he led strategic development and implementation in major policy areas. He was awarded a CB by the Queen in 2000 for his contribution to public service.

Peter has written a sequence of 24 influential leadership books. He is a Visiting Professor of Leadership Development at Newcastle University Business School and a Visiting Professor in the Business, Enterprise and Lifelong Learning Department at the University of Chester. He has worked with senior staff at Edinburgh University, the University of Brighton and Herriot Watt University, and post-graduate students at Warwick Business School and lectures regularly at Regent College in Vancouver. He is a Professorial Fellow at St John's College, University of Durham. He was awarded an honorary doctorate (Doctor of Civil Law) by the University of Durham in 2015 for 'outstanding service to public life and to the Council of St. John's College'.

Peter is a Reader (licensed lay minister) in the Anglican Church and has worked with senior church leaders in the UK, North America and Asia. In December 2016 Peter was installed as a Lay Canon at Guildford Cathedral in recognition of 'distinguished service to the Church and the community'. Peter chairs the Guildford Cathedral Council.

Peter's inspiration comes from long distance walks: he has completed 24 long distance walks in the UK, including the St Cuthbert's Way, the South Downs Way, the Yorkshire Wolds Way, the Yorkshire Dales Way, the Ribble Way, the Speyside Way, the St Oswald's Way, the Great Glen Way and the Westmoreland Way. Peter and his wife, Frances, have three grown up children who are all married, and four grandchildren.

TITLES IN THE **100 GREAT IDEAS** SERIES

100 Great Branding Ideas by Sarah McCartney

100 Great Building Success Ideas by Peter Shaw

100 Great Business Ideas by Jeremy Kourdi

100 Great Business Leaders by Jonathan Gifford

100 Great Coaching Ideas by Peter Shaw

100 Great Copywriting Ideas by Andy Maslen

100 Great Cost-cutting Ideas by Anne Hawkins

100 Great Innovation Ideas by Howard Wright

100 Great Leadership Ideas by Jonathan Gifford

100 More Great Leadership Ideas by Jonathan Gifford

100 Great Leading Well Ideas by Peter Shaw

100 Great Marketing Ideas by Jim Blythe

100 Great Personal Impact Ideas by Peter Shaw

100 Great PR Ideas by Jim Blythe

100 Great Presentation Ideas by Patrick Forsyth

100 Great Sales Ideas by Patrick Forsyth

100 Great Team Effectiveness Ideas by Peter Shaw

100 Great Time Management Ideas by Patrick Forsyth

FORTHCOMING TITLE

100 Great Leading Through Rapid Change Ideas by Peter Shaw